Language

CLEAR SENTENCES

Mechanics

Punctuation

Word Forms

Sentence Faults

The College Writer's Handbook

The University of California, at San Diego | *Suzanne E. Jacobs*

XEROX | *Xerox College Publishing,* Lexington, Massachusetts | *Toronto*

The College Writer's Handbook

and Roderick A. Jacobs

ACKNOWLEDGMENTS

Extracts. Pp. 46–47: Edgar S. Cahn, ed., from *Our Brother's Keeper: The Indian in White America*. Washington, D.C.: New Community Press, 1969, p. 102. Reprinted by permission of the New Community Press; Copyright © 1969 by the New Community Press. Pp. 50–51: Joe Benjamin, from "Children at Play," *The Listener,* Vol. LXXI (December 23, 1965), pp. 1021–1022. Reprinted by permission of Joe Benjamin; Copyright © 1965 by Joe Benjamin, P. 63: Malcolm X, from *The Autobiography of Malcolm X*. New York: Grove Press, Inc. Reprinted by permission of Grove Press, Inc.; Copyright © 1964 by Alex Haley and Malcolm X; Copyright © 1965 by Alex Haley and Betty Shabazz. P. 81: David Wagoner, from "The Words," *Staying Alive.* Bloomington, Ind.: University of Indiana Press, 1966. Reprinted by permission of Indiana University Press; Copyright © 1966 by Indiana University.

ISB Number: 0-536-00691-1
Library of Congress Catalog Card Number: 72-86513
Printed in the United States of America.

Preface

This handbook is intended to help college students with their course papers and examinations as well as with the regular assignments for freshman writing courses. It provides help for the general bread-and-butter writing that many students will have to do after college. Much of the handbook has been written in response to the authors' experience in a college writing clinic. It attempts to focus on those areas which students coming to the clinic found most troublesome—in particular, structure, clarity, introductions, and wordiness—and to describe them in terms found to be already in common use.

Like all handbooks this is meant as a reference book. The index, table of contents, and list of margin symbols will help the student writer find the pages where a particular skill or problem is discussed, whether it be "Commas" or "Confused Reasoning." Then he can make use of the advice at once in writing or revising his own work. In this sense it is something like a telephone book or a dictionary. Parts of the book can also be read straight through and used as a standard text, with students and instructor working together on the exercises.

The rules for punctuation, agreement, spelling, and other "mechanical" matters are placed at the back of the book, partly for easy reference and partly because the need for checking on them comes late in the writing process, after the writer has made all other revisions, and the paper is nearly ready for final typing. Closer to the front of the book are those skills needed earlier in the writing process—first organization, then sentence structure (as dealt with in "A Writer's Grammar", word choice, and a short section on wordiness. Footnotes and bibliographical form in the research paper section conform to the recommendations of The MLA *Style Sheet,* second edition (1970).

The most useful part for many college writers may well be the sample approaches, sample techniques, and sample papers. These provide no instant formulas for success, but they do show the beginning student, who may be unsure about what to say or how to approach a topic, the sort of writing that other students have done. We have found that they encourage students to convey their own ideas in their own way within the general limits of the course assignments or other writing tasks.

The grammar, based on transformational as well as traditional concepts, concentrates on the relationships between form and meaning. It is a writer's grammar, one that seeks to make the would-be writer aware of the alternative forms of expression available to him. The grammar provides explanations for some of the recurrent problems that plague many student writers: fragments, dangling modifiers, and monstrously complicated sentences. These newer concepts have replaced much of the material usually included in the grammar section of a handbook: history of the language, parts of speech, and verb conjugations.

The general emphases of this handbook are two: (1) A writing course should build on what the student already knows; it must stress his strengths rather than his shortcomings. (2) What the student has to say must be important to him. He must want to be sure that his writing works, that is, says what he means to say.

We wish to express our gratitude to a number of people who have read and commented on earlier versions of this text—to our favorite editor, Chris Jennison, to Fran Osborne, and to Christopher Reaske. But we owe a special debt to Timothy Gunn, who is the person really responsible for the section on mechanics, and who must have read nearly every writing handbook in existence in order to make the section as complete yet compact as it is.

Suzanne E. Jacobs
Roderick A. Jacobs

Contents

3

Mapping: a Way to Check Your Organization and Coherence

4

Sample Approaches and Papers

5

Research Papers

6

A Writer's Grammar

7

Word Choice 145

8

Mechanics 171

Some Preliminary Suggestions

1 AT THE BEGINNING, THINK OF WRITING AS SPEAKING

The first thing to conquer is fear of the blank page. If you can write down the thoughts in your head, no matter how garbled, useless, or wrong these thoughts may be, then you have at least accomplished Step 1 and should stop reading this item and go to the next one.

If a blank sheet of paper fills you with dread, however, or if it makes you feel tight in the area of the heart or suddenly hungry, then you might use one or more of the following gimmicks:

a. Imagine you are talking to someone about your topic. Concentrate on this conversation until you can actually hear the words. Write down what you hear.

1

b. If you're mathematically inclined or like to think in terms of maps or diagrams, then draw a picture or write a formula. Explain this to an imaginary listener and write down your explanation.

c. If it's difficult to start at the beginning, then start in the *middle* of what you want to say. (Also see p. 4: *Separate the Writing Task into Stages.*)

2 MINIMIZE THE AGONY

If you are past the stage of fear but still go through considerable agony in the process of writing, then you might do well to forget temporarily about writing well. Don't think about good sentences, exact words, spelling, or punctuation. Think about getting all the material onto the page as quickly as possible. If you find there are often long pauses between writing one sentence and the next, and your mind wanders off the topic, then give yourself a time limit, say half an hour for a page of writing. Set the alarm clock and promise yourself a reward for accomplishing your goal, even if you are not satisfied with what you have written.

3 FORGET ABOUT FANCY LANGUAGE

Many students honestly believe that they must imitate someone else's style when they write papers for college courses. All too often the result is that their writing sounds inflated and phony and the ideas themselves unoriginal. Feel free to be yourself when you write, to say what you mean in clear, straightforward terms of your own.

Unless you are already a fairly skilled writer, a Thesaurus may do you more harm than good. It may tell what a word means but not what context to use it in. If you are a reasonably competent writer, use it if it helps you recall a word you already know but have momentarily forgotten.

4 CONSIDER YOUR AUDIENCE

A general rule in writing is to find out who you are writing *for,* and then to imagine at every step that some member of this audience is sitting by your side listening, arguing, and question-ing. Assume that this person is willing to listen but rather slow to catch on. Many examples may be needed before this person can grasp a general idea. He has to be led, step by step, through a reasoning process because he cannot or will not make the logical leaps that might help him grasp your meaning. Such a reader—or listener—may lose interest if a general idea is repeated. He is likely to become bored and stop reading altogether if he cannot make connections between what you have said on paper and his own experience. Different audiences require different words, differ-ent kinds of concrete examples, different syntax or ways of order-ing the words, and sometimes even quite different content. But any audience is slower to comprehend your message than you may, at first, believe.

5 FIND OUT ABOUT THE MEDIUM

It helps a writer to know the medium he is writing for. Of course he will know whether he is writing an article for a maga-zine (say, *Consumer Reports* or *Playboy*), a letter to the editor of the *Los Angeles Times,* or a short manual of instructions for build-ing a canoe. In each case, the writer knows what kind of writing he should do, how formal it should be, and generally what sort of style his readers are used to.

A writer of course papers in the first year of college, however, is often totally in the dark about the medium of course papers. You may never have read any, may never have seen any pub-lished, and you may assume that the sole reader of a course paper is a graduate student grader or the course instructor. You may not be at all sure what style of writing your reader expects, or for what purpose anyone would read what you've written. You may assume that the grader is not reading your paper for information but rather for purposes of evaluating the work you have done; and this fact means that he's not really an audience at all but rather someone between you and your audience.

What can you do? First, you can become familiar with the me-dium of course papers. Look ahead in this book to the sample course papers for literature and history. Ask your professors to show you samples of course papers. Second, assume that your instructor or teaching assistant is not only an evaluator but also part of an audience made up of all the students who took part in your course as well as all the people who have done the reading you have done. Third, assume that what you write could conceivably be published in a student journal to be read by anyone, student or nonstudent, interested in the subject matter.

6 SEPARATE THE WRITING TASK INTO STAGES

For many amateur writers of course papers the following plan will be helpful:

a. Write whatever random notes on your topic you can think of.

b. Decide, after looking at your notes, what general statement the paper, as a whole, will make. This is often a personal response to the material—your considered view of it. It does not have to be profound, startling, or even very original. But it must be what you really think.

c. Make an outline, putting your notes in order. (See the discussion of planning and outlining, pages 30–31.) Your outline represents the structure your final writing will have.

d. Consider now whether your topic is too broad to be covered in detail in the amount of space you have; or whether it is so narrow that you will have to pad out your material to fill up the space. If it is too narrow, then decide what bigger or wider question your topic is part of, and take this as a new topic. (If you are in a real quandary, this is a good time to go see the instructor or teaching assistant.)

e. Write a first complete draft with all possible speed. (Don't do another version of your notes. Write complete sentences.)

f. Put the draft away in a drawer for at least two days. (Some people, when they take it out again, find it completely disorganized. If this is the case with you, consider what you have written as notes only. Start again at Step *b*).

g. Revise. Much of this book consists of suggestions for revision.

h. Type.

i. Proofread. If possible, put the paper away again for a day or so before proofreading. If this is not possible, try to wait at least an hour. As proofreader, try to imagine you are reading someone else's paper for the first time.

Because you know the content of your paper thoroughly, you will probably have a tendency to skim it when you proofread. You can force yourself to be more careful by reading the paper backwards, from right to left and from the last page to the first. You will be surprised at the number of typographical and spelling errors you discover.

Criticisms to Anticipate in Organizing a Paper

Problems like irrelevance, incoherence, and vagueness are, in fact, very often problems in organization. We list them here in the front of the book because they are among the problems you ought to look for in your own writing at the earliest stages of each piece of writing you do. With good planning on your part, they should never occur at all. The three sections following this one—*Organizing and Developing a Topic, Mapping,* and *Sample Approaches and Papers*—suggest ways of organizing papers so that such faults in structure can be avoided.

Vagueness

A writer who takes too little time to think through his subject matter is apt to present his ideas in a vague prose that all too often characterizes political speeches, as in the following paragraph:

> The problem of pollution is serious. Efforts have to be made to overcome it or the results will be dangerous. Because of our failure at all levels to come to grips with the problem and to meet it head on, its menace has grown. What is needed is a major effort to conquer it or life as we know it will cease to exist on this planet. Such an effort must take into consideration economic and human needs, but it must be put into effect without delay—student

The passage above repeats common slogans without any attempt to particularize them by referring, say, to particular rivers, sewage projects, or automobile exhaust restrictions. In the last sentence the writer gives himself a way out with his reference to unspecified "economic and human needs." The following paragraph is more detailed and more persuasive:

> The Mississippi River has been described as an open sewer, Lake Huron is a dead body of water, and orange trees wilt under the poisons hovering in the Los Angeles air. Yet industrial lobbying groups in the state legislatures repeatedly succeed in turning back the most reasonable attempts to remedy the problems. The 1972 campaign over Proposition Nine in California shows all the forces and counter forces in action.—student revision

Vagueness does not always represent a deliberate attempt to withhold information. Sometimes it occurs simply as a result of laziness. For example:

> Basically Henry's whole character and way of speaking involve a hypocritical type attitude to the responsibilities of power. Sir William Bradshaw is really the same kind of person although he is a psychiatrist and Henry is a king. So both show hypocrisy is typical in power.—student

The writer has not bothered to specify the evidence for his characterization of Henry and Bradshaw. What had these men done or said to make him think they were hypocritical? More detail of this kind would have given depth to the characterization, and it would probably have made the writer think of more intelligent things to say. At the moment the concluding sentence "So both show hypocrisy is typical in power" is unjustified. The word *so* is a claim by the writer that he has proved his point, when in fact he has offered no evidence for it.

Repetitiousness

College writing is often repetitious when the writer has failed to think out his ideas adequately before writing his first draft. He is doing some of the thinking as he writes. We use a student example here which is difficult to read, almost incomprehensible. This gross lack of clarity is common in such cases and explains why the repetitiveness is hard to spot.

> Explain the importance of Marshall McLuhan's ideas.

> There is a vast gap between the scientific technology and the educational process of today. There is a well-established case for the proposition that our electrical technology has resulted in a radical discontinuity in our society. The discontinuity exists because scientific technology of today is advancing with greater speed than the educational process. With this discrepancy in the educational process, there exists a discontinuity within the environment. I agree with McLuhan's position about the electrical technology of today.—student

The writer asserts that there is a gap or discontinuity of some unspecified nature caused by the fact that technology has advanced faster than education. The vagueness and repetitiveness reflect a general lack of control over the prose that results from the author's apparent unwillingness to think for himself, to really think about McLuhan's ideas. The writer did, in fact, after thinking a little more, develop the idea that schools are preparing children for adult life in a society which no longer exists. The discrepancy between their expectations as fostered by the schools and their experience outside the classroom has led to a feeling of being lost and helpless in a land of strange monsters. This, the writer said, was what he believed McLuhan was saying. Then, after some further explanation of the ideas, the writer provided examples of the problems McLuhan was describing and showed that McLuhan was indicating what might be done to modify education so as to prepare people more adequately.

Here in a longer piece of writing is the same problem that we saw just now. The writer repeats the same general idea without giving specific detail. The idea, even though it might be a good one for a paper, remains shallow.

Man was created and had dominion over all living things which inhabit the earth. But the pollution which he has made and his spoilage of nature raise the question of whether man has been just with regard to his control over living things. The necessity that man be able to control himself along with all other living things is immediate if he is going to be able to continue his and all other species.

Man's lack of control has led to much contamination of the earth, its waters and atmosphere. Nowhere on earth is there someplace which has not been affected or will not be affected by this contamination which he has produced. This contamination has caused the extinction of much wildlife and the ruin of an ecological balance in the environments of living things.

The extent of this contamination has caused an awareness of man's lack of control, and various campaigns have been started in an attempt to try and check this contamination. "Earth Day" and "Friends for a Better Environment" are just two such examples.

It is my belief that these campaigns have helped increase the awareness of the contamination. They have set up "reclamation centers" for the re-cycling of certain materials, which might otherwise add to the pollution. But with each day that passes, more pollution is contributed to the already plentiful supply. Because of this fact, man will eventually impose certain controls on himself for the sake of survival. Studies have been started and are still continuing into possible ways of stopping pollution.—student

Irrelevance

IRRELEVANT PHRASES

There are some phrases, familiar to most teachers of composition, which are almost always irrelevant or unnecessary:

> I enjoyed the story very much. It kept me reading at a fast pace.
> I agree with the quote above.
> What I want to bring out from this is . . .
> Thus I have proved/shown that . . .
> In this paper I will show that . . .
> Now I have given three examples of . . .
> Next is an explanation of . . .
> I am now going to prove that . . .—students

IRRELEVANT MATERIAL

The phrases above are irrelevant only in a superficial way. Usually the problem is more complex. "Irrelevant" usually means that part of the material is not pertinent to the argument being presented.

The writer in some way has failed to see the relationship, or show the relationship, between some part of the paper and the main idea of the paper. It is quite common for an irrelevant sentence to seem perfectly relevant to the writer because he has other pertinent information in his mind that he has not written on the paper. But once the writer is aware that for his reader certain material is irrelevant, he should either remove it or revise it so that it does bear on the argument at hand.

The phrases above, such as "Now I am going to prove that . . . ," are often intended to assure the reader that the writer knows where he is going. But such assurances should be unnecessary if the paper is unified and the development orderly and logical. Normally, student writers are faced with a title or topic within which fairly limited goals are set:

What does Margaret Mead mean by "culture"?

"The problem of the cities." Discuss.

Evaluate the contribution of Durkheim to sociological theory.

Discuss the adequacy of the Copernican view of the universe.

Compare the attitudes towards nature of the Hopi Indians with those of the white pioneers.

"The current conservation craze is dangerous from the long-term point of view." Discuss.

The goal of a paper for a literature course might be to discuss one particular idea, "power" for example:

Assignment: Both the play *Henry IV, Parts 1 and 2,* and the novel *Mrs. Dalloway* present interesting notions of power although they are quite different. Compare these notions.

Suppose that these passages are parts of such an essay. How effective do they seem to you? Which are relevant and which irrelevant? See if your judgment concurs with ours.

Passage A: Shakespeare has justifiably been called the greatest of all playwrights while Virginia Woolf is one of the most sensitive women novelists of this century.—student

(*True perhaps but probably irrelevant, even as part of the intro-duction.*)

Passage B: ''Power'' is one of the key words in modern thought as it has been throughout the ages. Both Shakespeare in *Henry IV, Parts 1 and 2* and Virginia Woolf in *Mrs. Dalloway* deal with the effects of power, but their treatment is very different. In this paper I shall try to examine the differences between their no-tions of power.—student

Relevant but says little. Repeats the ideas already stated in the assignment.

Passage C: Before I examine the notions of power in these two books, it is first necessary to go into their subject-matter. *Mrs. Dalloway* is about a woman who is waiting for the return of a man whom she almost married, Peter Walsh. He had been the one she re-ally loved. Instead she had married Richard Dalloway, a British member of Parliament, and they now have a grown-up daugh-ter Elizabeth. The book tells her thoughts about what she has done and about her meeting with Walsh. There is also a sub-plot about an ex-First World War soldier who still suffers from shell-shock.—student

Irrelevant. A plot summary, while it may be useful for under-standing a difficult novel, is distracting in a course paper. The writ-ing that people do about literature should be a response to it, a personal response, just as the remarks one makes to another per-son about a neighborhood fire are personal when both have been witnesses to the fire. Your audience, you can assume, has already experienced the literary work.

Passage D: Power, according to Webster's *New World Dictionary,* is 1. ability to do; capacity to act; capability of performing or pro-ducing;   2. a specific ability or faculty;   3. great ability to do, act, or affect strongly;   4.a) the ability to control others; b) legal ability or authority; c) a document giving it. The parts of the definition relating to this part are 3 and 4a with 4b also being important. King Henry has the ability to act and to con-trol others and he also has some legal authority although his right to be king is not a firm one since he seized power from the previous king. In Virginia Woolf's novel, the psychiatrist, Sir William Bradshaw, has power but it is not really legal au-

> thority. Mrs. Dalloway has little power of any kind and does
> not really want it.—student

Quoting from the dictionary is of little use here. The object of the paper is to define ''power,'' not in a dictionary sense but in a descriptive sense. The writer should describe what power consisted of and the way it functioned in the two literary works.

Passage E: Like the poet Sylvia Plath, Virginia Woolf killed herself. Her interests were very different from those of William Shakespeare.
—student

Details about the life of the author usually are irrelevant in an essay about the novels, plays, or poetry of that person. In this case the link is very strained, indeed, between the suicide of Virginia Woolf, the suicide of Sylvia Plath, and the notion of power in works by Shakespeare and Virginia Woolf.

Passage F: In both the play and the novel, ''power'' is presented as control over human beings by other human beings. For Virginia Woolf, power is horrifying. The psychiatrist, Sir William Bradshaw, who is really power-crazy, tries to control the shell-shocked Septimus Smith and eventually drives him to his death. Mrs. Dalloway herself, by refusing to marry Walsh who might have controlled her, has kept her freedom and her ability to live her own life as a human being, not a puppet. Shakespeare accepts power as not only inevitable but desirable if it is exercised with a sense of responsibility towards those controlled. Without authority and legitimate power, man does not know his place within the universe, and the kind of anarchy represented by Falstaff occurs. Virginia Woolf looks at power from within, from an individual mind seeking freedom from fear and interruption. Power is thus likely to be a menace. But Shakespeare looks at power from outside. He looks at the whole society of men and concludes that power, as manifested in legitimate authority, is necessary if men are to live harmoniously together.

Thus it has been shown that the notions of power are quite different in the two works discussed. Virginia Woolf sees power from the viewpoint of a person's inner consciousness—power is a dangerous force. Shakespeare sees power from the viewpoint of the society of men—power is a necessary force.—student

Relevant, but the last paragraph is unnecessary because it repeats the preceding one.

Passage G: I agree that both *Henry IV, Parts 1 and 2* and *Mrs. Dalloway* present interesting notions of power although they are quite different. It is not surprising that they are different because the works were written by two very different people. I think that Virginia Woolf, as a married woman, is naturally concerned about the repressive power that a husband can have over a wife. Shakespeare, however, does not come to grips with the corrupting power of the marriage bond in our civilization, probably because he wishes to maintain it.—student

Unnecessary first sentence. There's no need to inform the reader of your agreement. The rest is irrelevant because you are supposed to compare the notions, not to apply women's lib. judgments to the life of the writer.

Passage H: Although Virginia Woolf is a twentieth century writer, she is sometimes harder to understand than Shakespeare, who wrote in the sixteenth century.—student

Irrelevant.

Passage I: Shakespeare and Virginia Woolf are both concerned with the effects of power, but only Shakespeare is really concerned with the nature of power.—student

Good.

Passage J: Many Americans today are concerned about the power that others have over us. This power is not always properly managed or democratic. Shakespeare too, along with Virginia Woolf, writes about power.—student

First two sentences have not been *made* relevant, and the third really does very little to achieve the goals of the paper.

Incoherence (relevance in the paragraph)

A sentence within a paragraph may sound completely irrelevant or out of place. To the reader it seems totally unconnected, in any logical way, with the sentence that came before it.

To correct this, the writer has to remove the sentence to some more appropriate place or rewrite the sentence, making it fit the logic and ideas of the paragraph.

A paper on Zuñi marriage customs may quite validly include descriptions of the attitude towards adultery and of divorce procedures; but notice, however, that some of the sentences below interrupt the flow of ideas:

> **(1a)** Ending a marriage is not a very complicated matter. Adultery is not uncommon in Zuñi society. If a Zuñi wife is unhappy with her husband, she goes to a ceremonial fast in search of a new one. When she is sure she has a suitable husband, the old one will find all of his belongings on the doorsill. The rejected husband takes his things and goes back to his mother's house. Unfaithfulness usually does not break up a marriage. It is considered part of married life.—student

The sentence beginning "Adultery is not . . ." and the last two sentences have not been made relevant to the "ending-the-marriage" theme. The writer has not thought about the link between part of the material in the paragraph and the whole paragraph. The remarks about adultery could, for example, be tied in by grouping them together and linking them to the rest with a *but.* The result is a concession relationship conveying the idea, *Adultery may not cause divorce, but unhappiness may.* The paragraph is more unified, more coherent as follows:

> **(1b)** Adultery is not uncommon in Zuñi society, and even continued unfaithfulness usually does not break up a marriage. It is considered part of married life. But if for some other reason the Zuñi wife is unhappy with her husband, ending the marriage is not a very complicated matter. She goes to a ceremonial fast in search of a new one. When she is sure she has a suitable husband, the old one will find all of his belongings on the doorsill. The rejected husband takes his things and goes back to his mother's house.—student revision

In the following sentence the writer has focussed on the words "not new":

> The imposition of a wage freeze was not a new phenomenon to the growers.

The reader should expect the next sentence to explain why it was not new. But the student writing the paper wrote this:

(2a)   The imposition of a wage freeze was not a new phenomenon to the growers. Now they could save on wages while charging as much as they could get for their output. This was because the price freeze applied only to processed goods, not to agricultural produce.—student

The first sentence hardly fits in with the other two. They give a good reason for the planters to have been pleased with the wage freeze. The paragraph will cohere, or hold together, better if the first sentence is changed:

(2b)   The imposition of a wage freeze was not an *unwelcome* phenomenon to the growers. Now the growers could save on wages while charging as much as they could get for their output. This was because the price freeze applies only to processed goods, not to agricultural produce.
                                                                                —student revision

Had the writer wished to keep the emphasis on the fact that such a freeze was not *new,* she might have written something like this, which is also coherent:

(2c)   The imposition of a wage freeze was not a *new* phenomenon to the growers. A similar freeze had been imposed during the Korean War and a much longer one during the Second World War. But this one was more advantageous to the growers.—student revision

Overgeneralization

Generalizing is a legitimate part of the thinking process, but overgeneralizing is not. It is sometimes hard to determine just where the boundary lies between the two. Certainly the subject is worthy of discussion. If you are asked to criticize someone else's writing, for example, or to write a critical paper on a political argument in a news column, you might do well to examine the writer's generalizations. Is the evidence for them fair and representative, or does it consist of an arbitrary collection of isolated incidents? Does it ignore large numbers of people or important pieces of evidence?

A writer overgeneralizes if he says, "All textbooks are dull," because surely he cannot know about all textbooks. He knows only certain textbooks—those he has read or heard about from friends or even read about in other books. Omitting the word ''all'' is not much safer because

> Textbooks are dull.

really means to the reader that *all* textbooks are dull.

The same is true of phrases like *people in the North, the people of Switzerland,* or *blue-collar workers.* A writer cannot legitimately say

> Swiss people are friendlier than Americans.

However, he can say:

> The Swiss of my experience. . . .
> Most Swiss that I have heard about. . . .
> Very often I have found that. . . .

There is meaning to

> A little over 33% of blue-collar workers vote a straight Democratic ticket every time they vote.

so long as it is clear what a blue-collar worker is. Such a statement has presumably come out of a statistical study in which a little over 33% of those interviewed said, ''I vote a straight Democratic ticket when I vote.'' On the other hand, one can't really say:

> Seven out of ten Swiss are friendlier than Americans.

Friendliness is not the sort of concept which lends itself to statistical studies.

It is legitimate to make tentative generalizations so long as it is clear to the reader that the generalization is a tentative one.

> College students, I *suspect,* are no longer interested in knowledge as a reservoir of facts.

or

College students are *probably* no longer interested in knowledge as a reservoir of facts.

But the credibility of this kind of statement will depend a lot on the context: Does the writer seem to know what he is talking about? Is there enough detail about these "college students" in his other sentences?

Writers frequently generalize by citing one example as typical of a whole class:

Charles Harrison, living in a townhouse near the center of the city, knows he must lock and double-lock his front door. Living in the inner city all too often means living inside your own fortress.—student

But whether or not this is an overgeneralization depends on the circumstances. Some illustrations may not be representative. In such cases a hidden claim or premise is involved, one suggesting that such and such an event typifies a particular generalization when in fact this may not be so:

Any elaborate welfare system is dishonest and self-defeating. We find a strong, healthy man preferring to live off of others instead of working to support himself. Welfare gives him a way to do this. If there were no welfare, he would have no choice but to work. We need to get rid of welfare except as a very temporary minimal subsistence system serving to bridge gaps in employment supply and demand.—student

The healthy man cited above may perhaps be typical, or perhaps his case is an isolated one. The writer has omitted the crucial evidence on this point. Some social scientists maintain that by far the largest number of welfare recipients are children, invalids, and the aged. They say that others are families whose major wage earner has lost his job, exhausted all unemployment benefits, and can still find no work. *If* this is so, the writer cannot honestly say the healthy man is the typical welfare recipient. *If* these social scientists are wrong, the writer has to show that they are.

In any case, a writer should not use a single illustration to distort the general picture or mislead the reader. The single illustration cited below is not enough to establish the general idea. The use of a name and location should not blind the reader into assuming that the illustration is as representative as the writer implies:

> Students are graded not according to their competence but according to the political beliefs expressed in their papers. Stephen Crossland of UWM was given a C minus last December when he wrote a paper supporting our country's efforts in Southeast Asia. When he revised it and included a leftist condemnation of so-called atrocities, his grade was raised to an A minus. Moreover, all over the state new faculty are being hired on the basis of their answers to questions put by radical-liberal interviewers. I had one case of this less than a month ago at one of our most prestigious institutions. The situation in the universities is drastic, and drastic remedies are required.—adapted from a political speech

In the following paragraph the writer argues that Christianity is a religion less humane than the religion of the Aztecs. But notice that the evidence he chooses for comparison of the two religions is not really representative:

> The Christian religion is far less humane even than the religion of the Aztecs. Crusading Christian knights righteously slew pagan men, women, and children by the thousands. Fine upstanding Christian guards killed millions in concentration camps. The Aztecs only infrequently practiced human sacrifice. So it might be better for us all to adopt the ancient Aztec faith.—student

The writer has referred to only one cruel practice of the Aztecs, implying falsely that there were no others. The concentration camp example is weak; there is no evidence presented that the guards or their masters were following Christian tenets in their activities. More two-legged men have killed people than have one-legged men. This does not indicate that we all ought to give up one leg. If the writer is to make a good case for his initial generalization, he must show that the property of being Christian (rather than, say, the general property of political or religious fanaticism or of two-leggedness) is the one motivating the behavior he deplores. He might also seek to show that this motivation is not restricted to a specific historical period like the Middle Ages or World War II.

Oversimplification

Failure to think about details may lead to gross oversimplification of problems. A complicated set of events may be treated as if the events had but one cause, or as if there were two and only two sides to any dispute about them. For example:

> It is difficult for people like myself to realize what any type of racism is because I was raised with the idea that blacks, whites, reds, and yellows are all human beings. But many people must fight to conquer their discriminatory feelings.
>
> —student

In other words, the cure for racial prejudice is easy. Just raise your children so that they don't have it. An oversimplified problem is provided with an oversimple solution.

The author of the passage below has obviously thought little about the play he has to discuss. There are other facts about the play which should have shown the writer that his last two assertions are not only oversimplified but wrong.

> The basic problem presented in *Hamlet* is the hesitancy of the main character, Prince Hamlet. If Hamlet would take action without this unnecessary hesitation, the other problems in the play would give little trouble. Shakespeare's point is that some people are too hesitant.—student

A literary work, especially a major one, rarely has a single "basic" point. Nor is a complex social problem likely to have one simple answer. If you find only one, be sure to go back and look carefully again. Have you considered all the facts? Have you provided a "simple" solution which is really an impossibly complicated one? Are you treating as bad guys or good guys people who are really a puzzling mixture of good, bad, and morally neutral characteristics?

Confused Reasoning

A very frequent type of confused reasoning is the misuse of the cause-effect relationship. Sometimes a rather strict causal relation is implied between sentences, the writer claiming that something causes something else. Sometimes the link is so obvious as not to require evidence justifying it:

> The warm damp air rises to colder levels and therefore cools. The decreasing temperature of the rising air mass causes the vapor to condense into little droplets that may eventually become large enough to fall as rain.—student

> In that region the white churches reflected the racial values of the slave-owners supporting them, so that the blacks naturally preferred to form their own black churches.—student

But sometimes the link is not at all obvious:

> The growing interest in the environment has led to greater participation in snow-skiing and surfing. Consequently these activities have become the two most popular and enjoyable sports in the United States.—student

The first sentence claims a cause-effect relationship which is far from obvious. There is increasing interest in the environment. There is greater participation in the two sports. But the first phenomenon is not established as the cause of the second. Greater participation in snow-skiing and surfing does not necessarily cause them to become the most popular and enjoyable in the country. And how could the last statement be verified?

Some cause-effect relations may be justifiable, yet may lack adequate justification by the writer:

> The whole has now become separate political units so separate that each considers itself distinct. This is why there is war between these units.—student

The explanation here is inadequate. The second statement does not follow from the first. Not every political unit considering itself distinct from other units goes to war with those other units. Additional facts must be considered. Here the student writer has added more details to justify the cause-effect linking:

> The whole has now become separate political units, so separate that each considers itself distinct. Yet there are still areas of industrial regulation and taxation where jurisdictions inevitably overlap. If one of the units succeeds in getting these responsibilities assigned to itself, it will surely end up by dominating the other units. This is why there is war between these units.—student revision

Without necessary additional evidence, the passages quoted above become examples of an unjustified hidden premise or claim:

> Greater participation leads to the greatest popularity and enjoyment.

and

> Political units considering themselves distinct will war against each other.

The invalid hidden claims should be clear to you in the following pieces of student writing:

> The Pharisees followed all rules scrupulously. As a result, they followed the letter of the law rather than the spirit of the law.—student

> The least violent of all physical activities is physical conditioning. Being least violent, it is the most popular and important form of athletics.—student

Unfortunately, a concealed claim and the corresponding lack of supporting detail can be quite harmful, and may arise from deliberate dishonesty:

> The economic growth of Red China and the consequent endangering of our own welfare and freedoms is beyond argument. Anyone who does not believe that China has expanded her economic growth immensely has only to look at the gross national product figures below. Obviously we must prepare for the eventual struggle by selectively stimulating those defense industries that will be needed for conducting operations over huge land areas without adequate surface transportation facilities.—student

In the above passage the writer has attempted to conceal within his discussion the claim, unjustified by the passage itself, that China's economic growth must inevitably lead to war with us. But sometimes the hidden claims do not arise from deliberate dishonesty but from the substitution of slogans for rational thinking. The slogans may even embody partial or complete truths, but the user has not troubled to think them through or perhaps to verify them.

Undefined Terms

Faulty definition is more than a problem of a word or two. The writer quoted below should probably start over from the beginning:

> Those who live in America, even though they may not discriminate, still have a certain racist feeling because racism in America is institutional and has been since the slaves were shipped over from Africa.—student

What is "a certain racist feeling"? Does the writer intend to explain or define it? Does he really mean every person living in America? What is "institutional racism"? The term requires explanation if it is to be identified as the cause of the "certain racist feeling." Obviously the writer needs to explain what he means by *racism,* to show how this racism has been institutionalized, and then to show how such institutionalization conditions inhabitants of America to have the racist feeling he refers to but does not describe. If he does this successfully, he will have isolated targets for reform, replacement, or abolition. Having thought out the material in this way, he can then begin to outline his paper.

There are also other problems with definition. If the writer uses a term in a narrower or broader sense than the customary definition allows, careful definition is even more important than with little-known or little-understood terms. One surprisingly common problem is the use of a definition that runs quite counter to the way the defined term is normally used. The problem usually arises out of the writer's failure to consult a standard reference work:

> The basic concept of Liberalism is trying to reestablish the value and morals of the past.—student

Perhaps the particular values and morals referred to are ones that fit in quite well with traditional definitions of Liberalism, perhaps not. More validly the example above could serve not as an ordinary definition but as a surprise paradoxical assertion or redefinition to be justified in the rest of the paper. Unfortunately the rest of the student's paper indicated that he intended the above to be a normal, informal definition of Liberalism. As such, it will not do.

A FINAL NOTE

The eight categories used in this section describe eight major criticisms a writer needs to anticipate:

Repetitiousness	Vagueness	Confused Reasoning
Irrelevance	Overgeneralization	Undefined terms
Incoherence	Oversimplification	

To some extent they overlap. If you have spent too little time
thinking about your material or gathering detail, you will find that
you have committed more than one of the above errors, perhaps
all of them. Faults of repetitiousness, irrelevance, and incoherence,
the first group above, occur most often when material has not
been structured or arranged. Those in the second group—vagueness, overgeneralization, and oversimplification—are usually the
result of insufficient detail. Confused reasoning and undefined
terms (Group III) can be traced to errors in logic. This section has
provided descriptions of each kind of error. The next section is intended to help you plan and organize your writing so as to avoid
these errors.

Organizing and Developing a Topic

The Unifying Idea

Every piece of writing, if it is to be understood, has a central idea. Even a set of instructions for filling out an income tax return will communicate some main thought, such as *Don't make mistakes on this form,* or *It's important to do this form carefully.* Here are the central ideas from four other pieces of writing:

The graylag goose has elaborate courtship rituals.

Eustacia was selfish.

Justice can mean different things to different people.

Caesar was, in all, a fair man.

None of these ideas in themselves are very exciting. They all

25

sound vague, general, dull, and perhaps obvious. But then it is usually the detail, and not the general idea, which carries interest or excitement.

The unifying idea may be stated in the first sentence, the second sentence, any sentence of the first paragraph, or it may not be stated at all. A novelist or poet, even a writer of essays may write about characters, events, places, and feelings. Yet even for such writers there has to be an overall viewpoint or focus around which to organize his ideas. If not, there is nothing to explain why the writer chooses to include some kinds of detail and to omit others.

The scientist, unlike the novelist, will almost always state his unifying idea in some single sentence, probably in the opening paragraph, and perhaps more than once. An article might begin as boldly as this:

> Recent research has shown (*x . . y . . z*). I will argue here that the cause of these symptoms lies particularly in the diet of Western rural Americans.

(See *Beginnings,* p. 32, for more ways to state the main idea in the first paragraph.)

Whether stated or not, some sort of unifying idea is *there.* The reader senses it, and the writer, of course, uses it to give shape and coherence to the great bulk of his words and sentences.

The problem for the writer is how to turn a topic into a unifying idea. If you start with a topic like

A college course in writing

then you are obligated to say something about it. For example:

1. Here is a plan for *a college course in writing.*
2. *A college course in writing* should not be required here because almost everyone writes quite well.
3. The *writing course I had in college* was very practical.

4. Writing cannot be taught in *a college course in writing.*
5. *A college writing course* is a quick and frightening way of finding out exactly what one has—or doesn't have—to say.
6. *A college writing course* should teach students how to ask questions.

So the topic is what you write about, and the unifying idea is what you say about the topic.

Suppose for a paper on the novel, *Pride and Prejudice,* which you have just read, you were given the topic:

> *Mr. Darcy's pride*

The problem is to decide what your own feeling about this topic is and then to state your feeling as a unifying idea. For example:

1. Mr. Darcy's reputation for ''pride'' was mainly a creation of jealous, nosy townsfolk.
2. Mr. Darcy was proud in the sense of being reserved—appropriately reserved.
3. Mr. Darcy's pride changed to humanness, concern, and love.

If for a sociology assignment you choose to investigate *Occupations in California Chinatowns from 1900–1970,* then this area is your topic. But once the research is finished and you must write the paper, then you have to formulate a main idea, to say something about occupations in California Chinatowns from 1900–1970. Here are several possibilities:

1. People from California Chinatowns were excluded by law from certain jobs in the years between 1900 and 1970.
2. The skills many people learned from the Oriental cultures were not used for earning a living as much as they might have been.
3. The kinds of jobs held by people from Chinatowns in these years show a gradual but steady change.

This topic for a biology paper:

> *Our recent experiments on dentalium eggs*

might be transformed into this unifying statement:

> *The experiments on dentalium eggs* showed the exact location of
> the genetic material responsible for the growth of the apical tuft.

A unifying idea, unlike a topic, is a statement of some sort. It is often some kind of personal response that someone could argue with if he cared to. But responses can range all the way from very personal opinions to impersonal statements practically devoid of feeling. For instance, it is hard to disagree with anyone who says, "The graylag goose has elaborate courtship rituals," but at least it is conceivable to do so.

In writing essay examinations it is especially important to think in terms of the unifying idea. One student who failed to do so was asked this question:

> Some historians argue that the causes of the Great Depression
> were more psychological than material. Do you agree or disagree?

The student said he agreed. Then he gave the dates of the stock market crash, some facts about poor distribution of foodstuffs, and the failure of banks—none of which really argued for or against a psychological explanation of the Depression. What he said related to the general topic, the Depression, but it did not answer the specific question.

The writer might have argued that the Depression was not caused by lack of food or productivity (i.e., material things) but rather by too much optimism on the part of American businessmen, too little candor in criticizing business abuses, an unrealistic belief on the part of most Americans in a "permanent plateau of prosperity"—and, by contrast, a sudden loss of confidence in generally sound banks and people's fear of spending what money they had left. All of these factors, it could be argued, are psychological.

Examination questions often begin with the word ''Discuss.'' For example:

Discuss the concept of equality in Rousseau's *Social Contract.*

The word ''discuss'' is usually a signal which means:

Here is a topic.

Make a statement about the topic.

Provide supporting evidence for your statement.

The student writer given the question above decided to approach it by making her first statement a general definition of equality as Rousseau saw it:

What Rousseau meant by equality was that all men, regardless of appearance, culture, or the state of their civilization, were equal in that they possessed the same general rights and privileges.—student

After first naming some of these rights and privileges, the student spelled them out. She showed that in Rousseau's view ''uncivilized'' peoples and Western European ''civilized'' man, different as they might seem, possessed some of the same rights and privileges.

The same procedure can be used in discussing a long quotation. For example, suppose you were asked to write about some aspect of this quotation:

There is an ideal that has long been basic to the learning process as we have known it, one that stands at the very center of our modern institutions of higher education and that had its origin, I suppose, in the clerical and monastic character of the medieval university. It is the ideal of the association of the process of learning with a certain remoteness from the contemporary scene—a certain detachment and seclusion, a certain voluntary withdrawal and renunciation of participation in contemporary life in the interests of the achievement of a better perspective on that life when the period of withdrawal is over. It is an ideal that does not predicate any total conflict between thought and action but recognizes that there is a time for each.

—George F. Kennan, *Democracy and the Student Left*

In your essay you would have to deal with the central argument—that intellectual "thought" should not be undertaken at the same time as "action," possibly political or social action. But there are a good many approaches you could take, or, in other words, many different unifying statements you might choose to make. Here are a few of them suggested by student writers:

1. A modern university could model itself after the medieval university in ways that would allow for such seclusion. (Then a listing and description of these ways, followed by thoughts on how this seclusion would change qualitatively the kind of learning received.)
2. Thought and action must not be thought of as separate activities; without action, or experience, the thoughts a student has are of very little value or substance. (Then a listing of the kinds of worthless knowledge gained by those isolated from action or experience.)
3. The writer agrees: One is likely to have a better perspective on contemporary events after a period of secluded study and contemplation. (He then gives examples of contemporary events and the ways people who have acquired perspective from a period of academic seclusion would view those events.)

The Relation of the Paragraph to the Paper: The Plan or Outline

The first major task of the writer facing a topic is to select a unifying idea, a viewpoint on the topic. (See pp. 25–28 for discussion of this). Then he must decide how to deal with the idea, or what approach to take. Perhaps the idea will be stated first, or perhaps a necessary definition will be given. The remainder of the paper may be devoted to explaining, illustrating, or developing his idea.

You should—in your own way—write out your plan for the topic. An outline of this kind can take many forms. Some writers like to work out a neatly set-out outline like this:

> *Topic:* Local Control of Schools
>
> *Unifying idea:* Present methods of organizing and financing our schools do not provide for real local control.
>
> *Approach:*
>
> I. How the present system developed
>   A. Need for community integration
>   1. Schools organized to serve local community needs
>   2. Needs and policies defined by regular meetings of citizenry
>   B. Growth of community
>   1. Immigrant desire for upward social mobility

Other writers prefer a less formal way of sketching out their approach:

> I want to show that local control of schools is neither possible nor desirable.
>
> I'll start with a statement of present problems in the schools—dictation of requirements by state bodies, rejection of school bonds for financing schools, low status of teachers, irrelevance of curricula. Then I'll show how well the system worked in the eighteenth and early nineteenth centuries.

Whatever your approach, you need to break down the unifying idea of the whole paper into parts, perhaps into a number of narrower ideas or into a logical sequence of steps, or some combination of narrowing and sequencing. Each of the parts becomes the unifying idea of a paragraph, sometimes more than one paragraph. Each paragraph has an idea of its own. Sometimes a reader can summarize it; sometimes the idea is already stated by the writer in a single sentence, often called the ''topic sentence.'' The ideas expressed by each paragraph make up the whole unifying idea.

Paragraphs are thus the major units of a piece of writing. The purpose of this section is to suggest ways to develop ideas within the narrower framework of a paragraph. We start with two kinds of paragraphs that present somewhat different problems; paragraphs which begin and paragraphs which end papers.

Beginning and Ending Paragraphs

Novelists have often complained that the hardest task of writing any novel is figuring out how to begin. Other writers have the same problem. And endings seem almost as hard, since writers of articles and short papers are often tempted to end with some impressive-sounding phrases or else a boring repetition of what has already been said elsewhere in the paper.

BEGINNINGS

One favorite maxim for speechmaking was: ''Tell them what you're going to tell them, tell them, then tell them what you've told them.'' Speechmaking, however, is quite different from expository writing. A reader can always look back; a listener can rarely ''hear back'' unless he has a tape recording.

The length of the introduction—whether a single sentence or several paragraphs—is determined by the complexity of the material, the kind of audience one is writing for, and how familiar they are with the general topic. In the case of course papers, the audience is usually fully familiar with the general nature of the topic, and so little is needed by way of introduction.

The word ''beginning'' is perhaps better than ''introduction.'' The latter word suggests long and unnecessary openings like:

> People of all ages and climes have been concerned with the problem of . . . (whatever it is you are discussing). In this paper I can only deal superficially with a problem whose impact has been as stunning as . . . (some other impressive problem).

or the coyness of

Have you ever seen tomato plants in flower?

or perhaps the unattractiveness of

> In this essay I will give some causes of the 1812 War and then I will give some examples of why it was unnecessary. Then I will give some effects of the War and summarize.

The third of these beginnings is better as a plan of action for the writer than as an opening. It does, however, embody one essential ingredient of any beginning: it sets a direction. It is not an extra little decorative touch stuck onto the paper but the first essential step in the development of the paper.

Compare the following beginnings of a paper on the structure of the Chinese family:

First Beginning

The Chinese family consists of some sets of relationships with regard to tradition which have remained fairly constant. Many traditions, however, have been weakened and new ones have been formed to take their place. Two family types will be represented in this paper and their differences and the reasons for these differences will be the topic of this paper.—student

Revised Beginning

The complicated structure of the Chinese family has changed considerably in the past sixty years. The Lim family described by Harrison in 1918 lives in Shanghai but still functions like the rural peasantry of the previous six centuries. The T'sou family, reported on by Weinstein in 1970, functions more like members of an industrialized nineteenth century European society.

—student revision

The revised beginning reveals the writer plunging more directly into the subject matter of his paper. Parts of the first are a little too much like his private outline. It is wordy and boring to read. However, both beginnings show that the writer has thought a great deal about his topic. The following strongly suggests that the writer has thought little and does not yet know what he wants to say:

War is the topic. These two writers have expressed opinions and ideas. Each writer is convinced of his own opinion. They appeal to the reader's pity and sympathy. Some of what they say may be true; some may be untrue.—student

This version should be scrapped. The writer must first decide what he wants to say.

The kinds of beginnings are almost as varied as the writers or the topics chosen. If a writer has thought long enough about his topic and decided how he is going to develop it, then beginning should not be difficult.

BEGINNING WITH AN EFFECT. If he is using a cause-effect structure, he would do well to begin with the effect:

> Hikers in the southern end of the Appalachians have been noticing that treetops are turning brown and that once-solid rock surfaces are beginning to crumble.—student

> By the end of the 1960s, Indonesian children who had once spoken any one of fourteen different languages and dialects now spoke Bahasa Indonesia, a language that did not exist fifty years earlier.—student

BEGINNING WITH A "CONCESSION STATEMENT." The "concession statement" is a particularly useful opening when the author is going to explain something that might not easily have been predicted. The writer first concedes that something is commonly known or superficially true, then he proceeds to the more important statement. Notice how this procedure works:

> Although the universities were the scenes of intense political activism in the sixties, they did not alienate long-term public opinion as much as one would expect.—student

> Helping poorer nations was once the keystone of a liberal foreign policy. But today liberals seem to say, "Leave other nations alone. Don't interfere!"
> —student

> Despite the lack of population growth in this country in the last few years, consumption of non-durable goods almost doubled.—student

> The two works are concerned with notions of power, but the authors start with very different presumptions.—student

EXERCISE

Think about what must have followed these beginnings.

1. Perhaps the major problem this country has to face is the decay of the American city. If this decay is not halted, some horrifying possibilities await us. What is happening, what might happen, and what could be done?
2. Los Angeles has been called the America of the future. What Los Angeles is today, America will be tomorrow. A huge tangle of concrete freeways contains within it some ten million people, embracing Orange County in the south and extending to Riverside in the east.
3. In the last three presidential elections every major candidate has promised to help our cities. Yet almost no improvement can be detected. To understand why this is so is to understand something important about our system of government.

ENDINGS

Rarely is an elaborate "conclusion" needed, one constituting a major and important part of a paper. Sometimes it is as well to stop when you have finished what you have to say. If the focus of the paper is clear and the reader has understood the relationship of the ideas, then the ending should not have to tell him the point of the paper.

On the other hand, summarizing can be useful, even necessary, where very complex matters have been discussed in some detail.

In general, think carefully before ending with

1. a paragraph that summarizes or repeats what you have already said

2. a rhetorical question:

Is the youth of today going to allow such a takeover?

3. a row of dots:

> And so the wheel has turned full circle once more and . . .

4. an impressive quotation:

> The answer to the problems facing the present generation is not obscure. The prophet has written:
>
> > "Look within: thou art Buddha."

5. a suggested new direction or sudden change of attitude.

(Examples 1–4 are taken from student papers.)

EXERCISE

To help you as you go over your own papers, think about what must have preceded the following endings:

1. We will need a much clearer realization all around that culture *does* cost money and that it usually cannot pay its own way.
2. Mohican civilization had its own integrity and vitality. It was this that enabled the Mohicans not only to learn from the white man but also to add richly to the white man's civilization.
3. Sir Herbert Read said that education is the creation of happiness. The really creative work must be done to enable happiness to grow and flower in a child. The young delinquent, the maladjusted child, is just an unhappy person.
4. The more basic characteristics of U.S. television are thus quite distinct from those of the British network. By and large, these characteristics arise from one solid fact. Fundamentally, American television is controlled by three groups of people: the broadcasters who are concerned with making profits from advertising; the sponsors, who are concerned with making profits from the sale of cars, breakfast food and female toilet requisites; and the advertising agencies, who live off both. The yard-

stick for a program is still "Will it sell a product?" No one influential in either political party seriously questions such a
yardstick.

Idea Development Through Description

You can develop an idea by means of *description.* Notice the way
this writer piles one detail on another. Notice also the kind of detail he has selected. Together they add up to a central idea or a
unified impression:

> The Park Hill project is a particularly interesting development in large-scale hous-
> ing. Built in a slum area it stands on a sloping site so that the height of the
> building varies. It has elevators for vertical communication and decks for hori-
> zontal communication. These decks are wide enough for the movement of goods
> and furniture, for children to play in, and for adults to meet and gossip. All the
> front doors open onto the decks. They are, in fact, streets without fast-moving
> traffic. The recessed balconies and solid masses of pre-stressed concrete are inte-
> grated into a varied and exciting pattern.—student

The details provided in the passage above indicate that the writer
favors certain human values—the need and desirability of neigh-
borly intercommunication and the visual pleasures afforded by
skillful design—above, say, purely financial considerations. Description is more than just a pretty word picture of a landscape. It
may be a particularly powerful vehicle for important ideas.

You can use description more profitably in college writing than
you may realize. When an assignment calls for analysis, or when
you are asked a particular question in an examination, the bulk of
your writing can be descriptive, or a kind of descriptive definition
of a problem or situation. Suppose the question is

> What seems to you to be the most serious problem faced by
> urban schools?

You could select, say, the problem of student disabilities arising
from malnutrition and begin your essay by describing malnutrition.

Or suppose in a literature class you were asked

What was Huckleberry Finn's attitude toward the society in which he lived?

Your unifying idea, or the statement you choose to make, might be

The violence, false charity, and religiosity of the society around him are quite foreign to Huck, and almost certainly repellent to him. Yet whenever he encounters such behavior, he seems tolerant, even indifferent.

The writer could then *describe* in more detail Huck's tolerance, referring to particular incidents.

Or suppose the question was this:

In what way do automobiles shape our culture?

Then one answer might be

Automobiles determine the way we design and lay out our cities.

The writer could then *describe* typical city roads, parking lots and garages, service stations, advertising space and the size of it (big because of fast-moving cars), the layout of shopping centers. He might then contrast these with the amount of space given over to other functions of society such as recreation, farming, and housing.

Description is a powerful technique. Describing hunger in Ireland or the effect of napalm on a Vietnamese child may in itself be more powerful than marshalling arguments and reasons. Description, of course, serves other valuable functions. The workings of the automobile transmission system or the difficulty of learning Chinese can be described without necessarily implying moral values or arguing for a certain point of view.

Whatever the goals of particular descriptions, it is the depth of the description, the truth of it, sometimes the sheer amount of it that makes it powerful. To say, "Adolescence may be confusing and painful," is a bland, even trite, pronouncement. But a novel like Carson McCullers' *A Member of the Wedding* is neither bland

Illustration 39 ¶ **dev**

nor trite because it describes, it brings to life, situations that motivate such a statement. Here this author speaks of Frankie, also called F. Jasmine, a younger sister of the groom:

> She wanted to speak to her brother and the bride, to talk to them and tell them of her plans, the three of them alone together. But they were never once alone; Jarvis was out checking the car someone was lending for the honeymoon, while Janice dressed in the front bedroom among a crowd of beautiful grown girls. She wandered from one to the other of them, unable to explain. And once Janice put her arms around her, and said she was so glad to have a little sister—and when Janice kissed her, F. Jasmine felt an aching in her throat and could not speak. Jarvis, when she went to find him in the yard, lifted her up in a roughhouse way and said: Frankie the lankie the alaga fankie, the tee-legged, toe-legged, bowlegged Frankie. And he gave her a dollar.
>
> —Carson McCullers, *A Member of the Wedding*

EXERCISE

Think of descriptive details from your own experience which would develop the following ideas:

1. Parents are (are not) particularly perceptive about their own children.
2. The kind of housing available affects the quality of the life of the dwellers.
3. Some character in a novel, poem, or play seems very real.
4. Some particular location has in the past aroused particular emotions.

Idea Development Through Illustration

You can develop an idea by giving examples, or illustrations. Here the writer first states his general idea, then gives several illustrations:

> The previous elections were also a mockery of democratic processes. The administration, to ensure that the results were predictable, ruled off the ballot the most likely threat, the popular General Minh, and also the only avowed ''peace'' candidate, An Truong Thanh. The Tri Quang Buddhists were excluded as ''pro-neutralist'' and the entire trade-union ticket was eliminated because of faulty

certification of one candidate. When, after receiving the election returns, a committee of the Vietnamese Assembly recommended invalidating them, the decision was reversed under the eyes of a gallery containing armed members of the secret police. After the elections, the runner-up, like many others active in the campaign, was arrested and thrown into prison. He will probably die there.

—student

Note that the example, if it's well stated, can often communicate a general idea. In each of the items below, for instance, it's easy enough to tell what general point the writer has in mind.

    (1)   You can't put your purse down any longer without someone snatching it. Even my neighbors steal my potted plants.

    (2)   No one in Congress has less than a hundred thousand dollars in assets. I know of several senators who have spent a million and more of their own money to get themselves elected.

An alternative method of illustration is to begin with one very long example and then turn to the general points illustrated by the example. A discussion of inflation might begin with John H. Leeburger of Terre Haute, Indiana, who worked hard all his life and looked forward to the then-ample pension of $3,500 per year. Today he is spending his old age in the most degrading kind of poverty. Then, after some more detail, would follow a more general discussion of the nature of inflation. Here again the honest writer will take pains to ensure that his particular case is both representative and relevant. Notice how Lawrence Wylie in his sociological study, *Village in the Vaucluse,* uses a specific incident to illustrate community awareness of the family unit and the roles assigned within it.

. . . One day Madame Favre was sitting in front of her house sewing. Three-year-old Dédou, who was playing in the street, went too near the gutter and was about to get muddy. His mother looked up and called sharply to him:

"Dédou, you'll get yourself dirty. Get away from there!" Dédou was usually a docile child, but this time a naughty urge got the better of him. He looked up impudently and shouted:

"Why?"

His mother gave him a glance that he would remember and said through her teeth:

"Because I tell you to be good. Because you're the child and I'm the mother. Because we're not animals. That's the way it is! So!"

Madame Favre was not merely exerting her authority. She was unwittingly explaining that there was a principle involved in this situation over which Dédou had no control. He could only recognize it and accept it. She was explaining that both she and he were part of a family and that each had a role that must be maintained. She was emphasizing the importance of human dignity. She was saying that those were the facts, pleasant or unpleasant, and that his only reasonable course of action was to conform.

—Lawrence Wylie, *Village in the Vaucluse*

EXERCISE

In each case below think of one example which will develop the topic in an interesting and accurate way.

1. The effects of prolonged unemployment
2. The portrayal of marriage in family television programs
3. The social role of churches today
4. Speech patterns and employment

Idea Development Using a Time or Space Sequence

Perhaps the most common way to develop an idea like the following:

Christopher Columbus was in some ways an irrational man.

is to tell the story of the relevant part of Columbus' life in the order that the events occurred. Then in the last paragraph the writer might state which actions were rational and which irrational or partly rational.

Chronological ordering is, of course, a common way for novelists and historians to organize their material. But always there has to emerge some larger kind of pattern, idea, or feeling. If not, the listing of events can be boring and meaningless. Time-ordering, while it is used by almost everyone, is just a superficial device. The novelist uses it, but his real purpose is to recreate human experience in some full and rich sense.

When you use chronological order in your own writing, make sure that the events you write about are linked not only in a time sequence but in other ways as well. Perhaps the events illustrate a tendency, or show a contrast, or set up a causal link. When you write a paper about a novel or a play, it is especially important to make sure that you select details illustrating what you have to say rather than details which summarize the plot of the work studied. (See our notes on plot summarizing under *Irrelevance,* p. 10.)

Here is a legitimate use of a chronological technique to describe a whole cycle:

> Scientific knowledge of any group of related phenomena goes through a regular pattern. *First* there is a period of fact-gathering. *Then* appears a variety of different interpretations of some of the data. *Eventually* one of the interpretations is likely to become predominant; usually it drives the others into obscurity. *The next stage* is the concentration of nearly all scientific activity in this field within the framework of the victorious interpretation. *When, usually much later,* results are found which don't fit into the established framework, some scientists seek to revise or extend the framework. Others may challenge its basic principles and seek to establish newer and quite different modes of investigation.—student, on Thomas Kuhn's *The Structure of Scientific Revolutions*

If you are asked to describe a scene in some kind of spatial order, listing things as the eye would see them, make sure that your list of details is not a random one. If you use a space sequence, make sure that the places you mention contribute meaning to the paragraph. For example, in the following paragraph the *places* make the contrast clearer between *us* and *the Japanese,* between *the poor Japanese* and *the rich Japanese.*

> *In Japan* the government was growing increasingly suspicious of our motives. *In the cities* more and more workers were being dismissed while *in their country clubs* plump industrialists thought mournfully about selling their cabin cruisers.

EXERCISE

We stated earlier that events in a time sequence should also have some unifying principle or idea. What is the unifying idea in the following passage? What is the effect of the time sequence? What would be lost if these details were arranged in some other way?

> The explosion did not come until February. In December the police arrested several hundred "agitators". In January fifty members of the parliament were placed under house arrest for an undetermined period. On February 3, police armed with automatic rifles surrounded a public meeting in Parliament Square and ordered the crowd to disperse. Someone threw a firecracker, and immediately a shouted order led to a rattle of automatic firing. When the frightened crowd had disappeared, thirty-four bodies lay on the pavement, some of them children. On February 4, a state of martial law was imposed and tanks patrolled the streets of the city. On the fifth, the civil guard burst into Aguilla's apartment before dawn, dragged him out into the street, beating him ferociously, and threw him into an armored van. Two hours later, as Maria Aguilla led a procession of women protesting the seizure, members of the guard again fired, killing three. By noon the city was in an uproar. A mob had gathered at Villanella Park and was marching toward the palace, armed with shotguns, pitchforks, and axes. For once the militia retreated. At 12:15 two squads sent to stop the protesters refused to fire and joined the marchers. At 1:10 General Ibanez issued a statement raising the state of martial law and restoring constitutional liberties. But by 2:30 Ibanez lay in the Fuego prison while a battered but smiling Carlos Aguilla proclaimed from the palace balcony a new era of universal suffrage, individual liberty, and freedom from foreign domination.

Idea Development Through Definition

It is often necessary to define a term or a concept prior to using it. One favored method is a logical definition, which first puts the thing being defined into the context of a larger class with which the reader is presumed to be familiar. Thus, William James began "Psychology is the science . . ." The second step is to identify the characteristic of the particular thing that differentiates it from the other members of the larger class. William James' definition did this quite briefly:

> Psychology is the science of mental life.

Unfortunately some of the most boring student writing begins with formal definitions of this sort. In any case, a random examination of professional writing reveals few examples of development by formal definition. What is more common is a working definition, one that enables the writer to get on with his topic.

> The meaning of the term "conceptual thinking" must ultimately be conveyed by exemplification.—Stephen Körner, *Conceptual Thinking*

> Economics is about the everyday things of life; how we get our living and why sometimes we get more and sometimes less.
> —Gertrude Williams, *Economics of Everyday Life*

Sometimes a form of classification is used instead of the definition. The writer breaks up one large concept or class of things into two or more smaller ones:

> Roughly speaking there are two kinds of human thinking. There is *creative* thinking, based on imagination and insight . . . This kind of thinking follows unpredictable channels, and follows no fixed rules. There is also *routine* thinking, that requires no special talent to carry it out. It proceeds according to fixed rules and along a course that is easily foreseen.—Irving Adler, *Thinking Machines*

This can sometimes be both easier to write and easier to read than formal definition. Avoid the statement of personal inadequacy:

> "Imagination" is a very hard word to define. One of its meanings is the ability to bring an image into your mind.
> —Harris and Jack Cross, *The Language of Ideas*

Such a statement all too often suggests that the writer has not given enough thought as to how he will present his ideas to the reader.

Definitions, whether formal ones or working ones, are rarely truly objective. They reveal certain biases characterizing the writer's view of his subject. When in the nineteenth century William James wrote his excellent text, *Psychology,* the subject was hardly a science in the sense that physics or biology now is. His definition of psychology as the "science of mental life" reflects some wishful thinking.

In general, the writer who needs to define a topic or term prior to discussion would do well to use a working definition. Such a definition is most commonly used to clear the ground of any entrapping ambiguities and to set forth the area to be investigated. This student, for example, gives a working definition of "reality."

Reality in Films

Phrases like "stark reality," "real brutality," and "authentic!" appear in many advertisements for movies, both in newspapers and on marquees. But obviously *reality* means different things to different people, and here it must mean part of whatever it is that makes a film attractive to large groups of people. It is apparently not the kind of reality associated with documentary films. *Stark* reality would not likely be found in a film of an actual battle, an actual signing of a peace treaty, an actual marriage. It would not be found in a personal account of a flood by an actual eye-witness. Nor would this kind of reality be found in a re-creation of an actual event, in "The Last Days of Hitler," for example, which shows actors performing in what looks like a documentary film.

The kind of reality that draws crowds and creates excitement may be found in *The Godfather,* the story of a real underworld gangleader, both violent and tender, who was given a fictitious name—or in *Soldier Blue,* the story of a wild-west massacre of Indians by Yankee soldiers, which was also based on an actual account. Both of these films have some claim to historical accuracy, but it was probably the aspect of violence rather than accuracy which made them popular. Further, it was the explicitness of the violence which made them "real." The important questions for creating *stark* reality are not: Is there evidence that this happened? Were you there to see it? Have you got a film of it happening? Was this a likely or probable occurrence? The important questions are these: "Did it *show* the wound, *show* the needle, *show* the bullet, *show* the body?"—student

EXERCISE

Give working definitions for:

1. freedom of the press

2. conflict in a novel or play
3. culturally disadvantaged
4. group dynamics

Idea Development Using Cause and Effect

Organizing your material in terms of cause and effect is a useful way to develop ideas, especially for pieces of writing longer, say, than 500 words. This approach can be exploited in two basic ways.

A writer can explore causes or give reasons. How did something come about? Why? What reasons have other people given for what happened? Do you agree with their conclusions? What are your reasons, and how would you defend them?

Alternatively, a writer might ask himself the question: What are the logical results of the situation I have just described?

The following long passage shows how natural this kind of organization can be. First, the writer describes a lake and shows how it is being destroyed. (He breaks this part of the passage into four very short paragraphs.) And then with the phrase, "The trouble began innocently enough . . ." he turns to the deep-lying causes of the situation, going back into time and tracing events, one by one, to the present.

> *In a territory later called Nevada, a tribe of Indians—the Paiutes—owned a lake. The name was Pyramid Lake.*
>
> It was beautiful—much larger and more scenic than its famous neighbor, Lake Tahoe. Captain John Fremont "discovered" it "set like a gem in the mountains" in 1844, when the waters and banks were prosperous with fish and wildlife. Anaho Island off the northern shore served as a pelican rookery. Geysers, hot springs and rare oolitic sands were nearby, and the last of a species of prehistoric fish, the *Cui-ui,* swam unmolested.
>
> Pyramid Lake was deeded to the Paiutes, a conquered people, in 1859. The white man had no need for the lake, and the land around it appeared worthless.
>
> *Today, Pyramid Lake is in danger of disappearing from the earth. The Paiutes are fighting both for its survival and their own.*
>
> The trouble began innocently enough. Control over Indian affairs shifted from the War Department to the Department of the Interior in 1859. In the early

1900's a new philosophy of conservation became Governmental policy. Interior was charged with special responsibility for conserving our country's precious natural resources and its scenic wonders. In the name of conservation, strange things started to happen. But they did not become visible immediately.

Irrigation was gaining use in the Western U.S. during the same period, and in the early 1900's, Interior dammed the Truckee River just above Pyramid Lake to divert water for the Newlands irrigation project. It was supposed to make cultivable some 287,000 dry acres, but in 65 years it has accomplished only a fourth of that—and the acreage proved to be inferior for farming and ranching. It takes twice as much water as is legally permissible to serve the land, largely because the irrigation ditches are unlined and 65 per cent of the water leaks out or seeps away.

Around 1930, the Indians found there were no more trout in Pyramid Lake. Water from the river had been diverted so that trout no longer could swim upstream to spawn. The tribe began legal efforts to regain the water, which had been diverted or appropriated without consultation. A few BIA officials sympathized and tried to assist the Paiutes but were fired or "promoted" away from Nevada.

—Edgar S. Cahn, ed., *Our Brother's Keeper: The Indian in White America*

The writer must make it clear to the reader that something is the cause of something else, or the effect of it, but usually this is not difficult. For instance, in each of the following sentences two things are happening, and it is clear that the first is the cause of the second:

When a neutron hits a chunk of fissionable material larger than the critical size, the chunk develops a chain reaction releasing enormous amounts of energy.

A drop in dollar spending and a fall in farm prices is likely to be followed by pressure on the government to increase subsidies and absorb surpluses.

A woman who is mercilessly exploited by her husband may take refuge in a neurosis if her disposition admits of it.

But occasionally it is better to use certain linking words to put a more explicit emphasis on cause:

This collision *causes* the release of enormous amounts of energy.

Because of the drop in farm prices, pressure was exerted on the administration to absorb surpluses.

His merciless exploitation of his wife *led her to* (or *made her*) take refuge in a neurosis.

Sometimes the focus is on the second event, the effect or result rather than the cause:

The major event was Johnson's resignation. *Consequently* the already disunited party was shattered into four or five competing fragments. The *result,* Republican victory, was inevitable.

Three events—the resignation, the shattering, and the Republican victory—are linked by a cause-effect chain. But the focus is more on the *effect* of the earlier event rather than on which events caused what. Linking words which focus on effect include:

result	it follows that
consequence	necessarily
effect	therefore

Your own feel for words must tell you whether such words are best included or omitted in any given situation.

EXERCISE

For each of the following name two possible causes.

1. Demonstrations became more violent (or less common).
2. Foreign cars became more popular.
3. She became even more shy in the presence of men.
4. The President became very popular with students and workers, but big business remained hostile.
5. Private schools became more common, while public education decayed.

For each of the following name two possible effects.

1. Legislation was passed forbidding the emission of any harmful gases.
2. Each year the universities poured forth thousands of graduates for whom there were no jobs.
3. Educators had to guarantee in advance specific results that their students would achieve.
4. Drugs shown to be physically harmless were legalized.
5. Fish, meat, fruit, cereal crops, and vegetables provided a steadily diminishing proportion of the human diet.

Idea Development Using Comparison and Contrast

One excellent way to develop an idea is to set up a comparison between two things. Ask yourself, "What property do two things share? In what way are two things different?" (Comparison refers to similarities, contrast to differences. But *compare,* when used without *contrast,* frequently refers to both similarities and differences.) Comparing and contrasting may be used on practically any level. A comparison can work inside a single sentence, it can be the structuring device for a paragraph, or it can be the unifying idea of a whole paper.

Here are examples of comparison and contrast inside sentences and inside a paragraph:

My brother is not only cleverer than I am, but also he has many more friends. He must, then, be out of my way before the old king dies.—student

Like the American Indian the Australian aborigine lost his culture and lands under the overwhelming impact of the aggressive white invader.—student

The Maoris were more fortunate in retaining land-ownership rights than their Australian cousins were.—student

In his book, *Slavery,* Stanley Elkins reports that for the black child the plantation offered no really satisfactory father-image other than that of the master. In the vastly more horrifying German concentration camps of World War II many of the inmates did not hate the SS. In fact, they often sought to persuade themselves that the guards were hiding benevolence under the mask of a cruel father. The camp inmates, dependent on the guards for life, food, warmth, and security took on the role of children, and were prepared to be loyal, docile, lazy, playful and silly, just as children are. Likewise, a full-grown black man was a "boy" until he was sufficiently aged to be labeled "uncle."—student

Note that in his comparison, Elkins is not reported as claiming that the American plantation was basically the same as a Nazi concentration camp. Instead, as he himself wrote, the concentration camp was "a special and highly perverted instance of human slavery."

Comparison and contrast can be an excellent way to define informally and to emphasize a particular characteristic. The writer of the following piece, for example, emphasizes a particular aspect of children's play by skillfully combining two sets of contrasts with a cause-effect relationship. The first contrast is between two types of children's street play in London. One is accepted by adults, the other strongly discouraged. But an outside event, a world war, causes a change in adult attitudes. The contrast is now between the present attitudes of parents towards a particular kind of play and the attitudes of prewar parents.

[Children's games in prewar London] presented us with opportunities to help and play a part in the work of the community. It was play for us to shop for neighbors, to help the milkman on his rounds by leading his horse-drawn milk-cart or pushing his float and measuring the milk from the huge churns. And it was play, for those of us fortunate enough to be on good terms with a shop-keeper, to make paper twists or funnels and sell broken biscuits from large crumb-filled boxes.

Some other forms of street play were not looked at in such an approving way by our elders. Floating bits of wood along rain-filled gutters, playing in derelict houses, lighting fires and building dens on vacant sites were regarded, perhaps rightly, as undesirable and to be stopped. They presented hazards, could be dangerous—and adult society, in its wisdom, did its best to interfere and discourage us. What was not recognized then was that, like children everywhere, we were imitating what adults did, and preparing ourselves for a social existence in a way that would have been impossible had we been confined to 'safe' play. But this was before the war.

The bombing of our cities during the war provided the next generation of children with exciting but even more dangerous sites on which to play. Fortunately the time had produced a new generation of parents, too; at least some of whom were enlightened enough to realize that this sort of risk-taking but basically creative play was not only more enjoyable to a child but also rather more encouraging of development than any of the 'safe' play they could so easily have imposed. Out of their permissiveness and the still undeveloped ideas of a few 'cranks' who had taken the trouble to think about the place of play in children's lives was born the adventure-playground movement.

—Joe Benjamin, "Children at Play," *The Listener*

The children's games during and after the war did not differ crucially from the prewar ones. Here the writer has focused on the likenesses. But now the attitudes of parents towards children's games are very different; therein lies the contrast.

Below is another example of comparison and contrast. The student first points out the likeness, even if it is superficial, between characters in a play of Brecht's. Galileo the astronomer looks up at the skies, so, he notices, do the dockworkers. But the student who wrote the following comment perceives that what is important is not the actions compared but the motives behind them. Thus, at a deeper level, Galileo is quite different from the dockworkers.

Galileo and His Countrymen

In the beginning of the play Galileo is excited by the social context of his research. He sees his discoveries, which challenge antiquated beliefs, as part of a social movement by which both workers and intellectuals will benefit. "At last," he says, "everybody is getting nosy. I predict that in our time astronomy will become the gossip of the market place and the sons of fishwives will pack the schools." He relates himself to the workers; like him they have discovered that there are contradictions between their observations of the universe and the ecclesiastical concept of the order of the universe. He tells the monks that even unread sailors and carpenters, not afraid to use their eyes, are discovering new ways of doing things.

But Galileo fails to consider that behind their similar discoveries there is different motivation. He is motivated by curiosity to study the sky, whereas the dockyard workers have jobs in which they are forced to view the sky. Whereas Galileo seeks to find the knowledge he acquires, the workers receive it without seeking. Excited by the fact that they have arrived at similar observations, Galileo falsely concludes that the workers are motivated by the same driving curiosity which motivates him—"that same high curiosity which was the true glory of ancient Greece."—student

Below are suggestions for ways to use comparison and contrast in your own writing. Where we say "compare," we could easily add "and contrast."

1. Contrast what is true with what is not true.
2. Contrast appearances, behavior, attitudes.
3. Contrast different methods of attaining the same result.
4. Contrast the apparent with the real, or the superficial with the deep, the fake with the genuine.
5. Compare motives. The same motive might result in different acts, one perhaps subtle and another crude. Or different motives might produce similar behavior.
6. Compare your own view of something with someone else's view of the same thing.
7. Compare the present with the past, one place with another.
8. Contrast a person's specific goal with the means he uses to attain it.
9. Contrast the potential and the actual. (Contrast, for example, what might have happened with what is happening, or contrast a man's intentions with his deeds.)
10. Contrast the severity, the extent, or the degree of two things.
11. Compare the conclusions reached by two different people. Compare the evidence they used. Compare the values or basic assumptions underlying their arguments. Have they used the same evidence but arrived at different conclusions? Are their conclusions the same in spite of different evidence? Examine the reasons for such discrepancies.

EXERCISE

Give examples of the way comparison or contrast could be used to develop the following topics:

1. the fairness (or unfairness) of our education system in meeting the needs of different Americans
2. a discussion of two works by the same poet, playwright, or novelist

3. an evaluation of the work of two Presidents
4. two theories about some area of science

Idea Development Using the Concession Relationship

You can also develop your idea by using details which seem almost to contradict it. Frequently you must do this in order to present an accurate account or description. You must concede that certain things are true, and then show that these facts, on balance, are less important than or subordinate to other facts. Below we underscore the more emphatic part of the statement. The other part is the concession, or the point which the writer concedes.

> **(1)** Although he was pale and sickly, <u>he could be aggressively courageous when courage was needed.</u>

> **(2)** Despite their shortcomings with respect to enforcement, <u>the consumer protection laws played the major role in undermining the old let-the-buyer-beware attitude.</u>

His self-respect and pride no doubt prevented Ishi from acquiring a more rapid and facile command of English . . . But these character traits seemed not to have <u>seriously cut him off from the people and activities he valued</u> . . .

—Theodore Kroeber, *Ishi*

Notice that some words serve to subordinate an idea, to make it the part which the writer concedes, words like *although, despite, even though, in spite of,* and *admittedly.* Other words serve to emphasize the stronger idea: *but, however, nevertheless,* and *yet.*

On a larger scale the concession relationship may be exploited, often quite effectively, as an argumentative technique. The writer first ''concedes'' all the major counterarguments against the argument he wishes to support. If he is dishonest or negligent, he may omit some of the most crucial counterarguments, but this lays him open to devastating refutation. This counterargument stage might be called the ''although'' section.

Then, in what might be termed the ''nevertheless'' section, the writer marshalls his own arguments and perhaps undermines a few of the ''although'' counterarguments.

For example, in a paper seeking to present in a more favorable light the Castro regime in Cuba, a student began by describing the stream of refugees leaving Cuba weekly, the one-party system, the mass executions at the onset of the revolution, the ineficiency of many parts of the administration, the decay of industries which had once flourished, the stifling of dissent among the peasants as well as among poets and artists. This was his ''although'' section.

Then he went on to place all the aforementioned in a ''proper perspective,'' as he saw it. He described even worse conditions under earlier regimes supported by the United States—executions without trial by secret police and right-wing vigilante groups, massive corruption, starvation, disease, and a deliberate use of irrational terror to render the population more submissive. The industries which had once flourished had exported most of their profits to the United States and were now languishing under an American-sponsored boycott. The peasants, though hardly overfed, no longer had to fear starvation or irrational terror. Corruption was rare, and people felt they had a voice in the future. The writer detailed further improvements and explained that earlier excesses had not continued. He concluded with a plea for our understanding and sympathy, combined with a condemnation of those who preach against left-wing dictatorships in Cuba while arming and financing right-wing regimes elsewhere in the Americas and in Asia.

When you organize a paper in this way, make sure that your reader can follow your line of argument throughout. Readers frequently complain (especially about student papers) that the writer has jumped the fence in the middle of the essay, arguing first for one point of view and then for the opposite one. The writing, they say, lacks a sense of conviction. It is all right to be impartial, but one should not change his mind in the middle of a piece of writing.

The following paragraph reveals a student too obviously sitting on the fence. The paragraph fails as a unified paragraph because the writer seems to be reaching two mutually contradictory conclusions at the same time:

A national health plan would thus improve the general health of the population without really adding much more expense than the present unfair system. Government regulation could lead to too much red tape and doctors would strongly oppose government "interference."

The writer *asserted* certain things when he should have *conceded* them. By rephrasing his sentences (using words like "although") he can produce a paper with the consistent point of view which had been lacking before. Think of the problem in this way: you cannot believe at one and the same time both that it would be better (1) to have a national health plan *and* (2) it would *not* be better. But you can see simultaneously both its advantages and disadvantages. Such insight does not prevent you from holding an opinion on the matter; it will simply make your opinion better informed. You are *for* something in spite of its disadvantages, or *against* it despite its advantages.

EXERCISE

Join each pair of sentences together, subordinating one and thus emphasizing the other. Then reverse the procedure, rewriting the sentences so that the emphasis is reversed.

1. Many Americans are poor. The U.S. is the richest country in the world.
2. This novel deals with social issues. It is about the emotional development of a family.
3. The atom is tiny. It contains enormous power.
4. Carrot juice contains little or no protein. It is rich in vitamins.

Take the two sentences you have written for (1), (2), (3), or (4) above. Examine the two carefully and think about their meaning. Then describe topics for which: (1) your first sentence of the pair would be a more appropriate opening than the second, and (2) your second sentence would be a more appropriate opening than the first.

Mapping: A Way to Check Your Organization and Coherence

In an earlier discussion of *Incoherence,* p. 15, we used a student paragraph on Zuñi customs. The writer, explaining how a Zuñi woman arranges a divorce, suddenly introduced an apparently different topic. In fact there was a close link, but the writer had not taken the trouble to explain what the link was. So the reader, following along the logical line of the writer's thinking, came suddenly to a break in the logic.

The mapping procedure on the next page is a way of finding breaks, if there are any, in your own paragraphs. It is a way of checking your work. It requires, first, that you work out the main idea and, second, that you show what each sentence does in the paragraph: Does it describe? Illustrate? Give a cause or reason?

Show contrast? If you can work this out, you will have shown that there are idea links, which a reader should understand, between one sentence and the next and between each sentence and the whole. If you cannot, then it is likely that something is wrong with part of the paragraph. Maybe a sentence should be left out, or perhaps rephrased, to make the idea link more obvious to the reader.

We illustrate the mapping with seven idea links:

description	cause (or reason) and effect
example or illustration	comparison and contrast
definition or classification	concession
time/space sequencing	

You are free to modify these or add your own terms. Invent terms of your own if these will help you think, really think, about the logical connection between your sentences.

To make the map, work out first the main idea of the paragraph, which might be stated in Sentence 1, or Sentence 2, or implied by the paragraph as a whole but not stated.

1. Write out the main idea in your own words, even if you have to oversimplify.
2. Then look at the first sentence and decide how it is linked to the main idea: Does it describe it, illustrate it? Is it a contrasting idea? Is it a reason or cause connected with the main idea?
3. Do the same with the second sentence. How is it linked to the main idea? Is it linked to Sentence 1 in some way? (See example below.)
4. Draw arrows to show the links, as suggested by the example below.

The paragraph on the following page was taken from the middle of a student paper on the topic of civil service examinations in China. The question raised about the topic was rather interesting because it involved general questions about all tests:

Do you think the old Chinese examinations were a good way of finding able and competent civil servants?

The student's general response, her unifying idea, was

No, they were *not*.

> [1] The exam was a test of irrelevant kinds of knowledge and skills. [2] It covered a person's knowledge of the Confucian classics. [3] Often the writing of poetry was also an important item on the examinations. [4] While possessing this knowledge certainly never hurt anyone, it seems strange that matters such as economics, accounting, and general administrative procedures never appeared on the tests. [5] A comparable procedure would be to test Americans on all of Shakespeare's writing before putting them in charge of our Post Office system, or perhaps before making them judges. [6] In China, as a consequence of knowing little or nothing about practical matters of business and law, the magistrates and other officials were forced to rely upon their secretaries, clerks, and servants in order to accomplish their jobs. [7] This would sometimes lead to further corruption in the system if one of these people decided to work things for his own personal gain.—student

Main idea: The examinations were not a good way of finding able and competent civil servants.

Cause: [1] Exams tested for irrelevant skills.   (This is why examinations were not a good test.)

　　　Examples: [2] Confucian classics   (Examples of irrelevant skills and knowledge.)
　　　　　　　[3] poetry writing

　　　　Contrast: [4] Knowledge of economics, accounting, general administrative procedures   (Relevant skills, contrasting with irrelevant skills.)

　　　Comparison: [5] Testing Americans on Shakespeare before making them post office administrators or judges   (Irrelevant skills, like the ones above.)

Effect: [6] Magistrates forced to rely on subordinates.   (An effect of possessing irrelevant skills.)

　　Effect: [7] Subordinates could indulge in corruption.   (An effect of having no skilled supervision.)

The diagram or map is one way of showing the idea relationships of the paragraph. The drawing of the arrows and the naming of the parts, as well as the degree of complexity, may vary slightly from one person to the next, but the process is the same for all: finding the idea relationships between sentences and between each sentence and the whole paragraph. Once you can accomplish this kind of task with other people's prose, and especially with your own, your reader should be able to follow you easily from one sentence to the next. When you do longer pieces of writing, it will be helpful to work out the links not between every sentence but between paragraphs.

You can also use mapping to help you read complicated articles or textbooks: find the links between paragraphs, or between one group of paragraphs and another, and decide how each part is linked to the main idea. By doing so, you can grasp the structure of the article. As a consequence, the material of the article will be much easier to remember.

EXERCISE

Another paragraph is mapped out below, this one a narrative paragraph. As the map is worked out here, it shows not the superficial time sequence but rather the underlying causes and effects. This is one version of the map; other versions are possible.

Study this map, and then work out in similar fashion a map for each of the paragraphs which follow it.

¹ When we first moved into our house seven years ago, there were only about eight families on the block. ² The area had originally been a tomato patch, but now it was a new subdivision with new houses and the realtor had said that we were a safe distance from Logan Heights, the black area. ³ In the next couple of years most of the houses on our block were sold. ⁴ Then it happened. ⁵ A black family moved into the neighborhood. ⁶ Panic immediately struck the neighboring families, including ours.

⁷ Until then, I had never come into contact with a black person. ⁸ All I knew was what white people had told me about them. ⁹ And as a kid I had soaked every word of it up. ¹⁰ So, before ever

knowing a black person, I already had in my mind an opinion that he was a no good so and so, and that he would slit my throat if I didn't stay away from him. [11] This, I'm sure, was the feeling of many of the white families on the street. [12] In the eyes of the whites, this one family of blacks made the neighborhood a black town, and their property values would drop. [13] So, what did they do? [14] The whites moved out and the neighborhood got blacker and blacker. [15] Pretty soon, our family really got scared. [16] We didn't go outside at night for fear that we would be jumped by one of them.—student

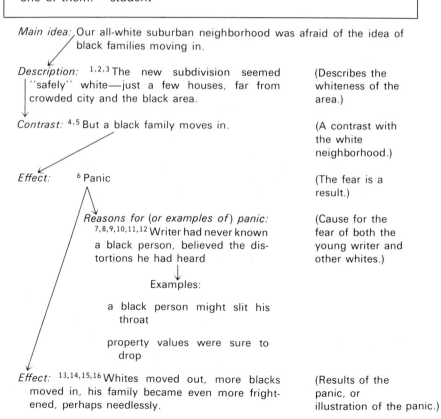

Main idea: Our all-white suburban neighborhood was afraid of the idea of black families moving in.

Description: [1,2,3] The new subdivision seemed "safely" white—just a few houses, far from crowded city and the black area.

(Describes the whiteness of the area.)

Contrast: [4,5] But a black family moves in.

(A contrast with the white neighborhood.)

Effect: [6] Panic

(The fear is a result.)

Reasons for (or examples of) panic: [7,8,9,10,11,12] Writer had never known a black person, believed the distortions he had heard

(Cause for the fear of both the young writer and other whites.)

Examples:

a black person might slit his throat

property values were sure to drop

Effect: [13,14,15,16] Whites moved out, more blacks moved in, his family became even more frightened, perhaps needlessly.

(Results of the panic, or illustration of the panic.)

1. I'd like to mention here that it is unwise to expect your company meals to look precisely like the company meals you see in the full-color food spreads everywhere. In this connection, I have news for you: food photographers do not play fair and square. It was once my privilege to watch a beef stew being photographed in the studio of a major food photographer. It was a superb stew—the gravy glistening richly, the beef chunks brown and succulent and in beautiful juxtaposition to the bright carrots and the pearly onions. I can make a respectable beef stew myself, but my gravy is never that gorgeous, and my onions invariably sink as though torpedoed. I inquired about this and discovered that the gravy had been dyed, and the onions had been propped up on toothpicks! Moreover, that very same morning, they told me, they'd had to lacquer a lobster.　　　　　—Peg Bracken, *The I Hate to Cook Book*

2. "The great object of life," Byron wrote, "is sensation—to feel that we exist, even though in pain. It is this 'craving void,' which drives us to gaming—to battle, to travel—to intemperate, but keenly felt, pursuits of any description, whose principal attraction is to the agitation inseparable from their accomplishment." And Stendhal confirmed him when he said that an age of revolutions and wars gives a "continual thirst for strong emotions. When they subside for a while, boredom follows until they rise again." We are enough in the same situation today to make an interest in Byron revive.
　　　　　—V. S. Pritchett, "The Craving Void"

3. A poll of students will show that they are not very sure about what their own family incomes really are. Usually it turns out they have a slightly exaggerated notion of their fathers' earnings. And despite the recent (quite justified) claim of a prominent clubwoman that "women spend 70 per cent of the national income, and we soon hope to get hold of the rest," an astonishing number of wives have no conception of their husbands' paychecks. In addition, there are some people so inept at keeping records and with such variable earnings that they do not themselves know how much they make. Even where income is known within the family, there is a quite natural reticence to reveal it to outsiders; thus investigators who made a 1939 survey of the birth-control habits of native white Protestants of Indianapolis often found it harder to get financial data than intimate personal information.
　　　　　—Paul A. Samuelson, *Economics*

4. Now it may seem paradoxical and illogical, but I make a distinction between lying and being dishonest. You can be honest and yet a liar—that is, you can be honest about the big things in life although sometimes dishonest about the lesser things. Thus many of our lies are meant to save others pain. Truth-telling would become an evil if it impelled me to write, "Dear Sir, your letter was so long and dull that I could not be bothered reading it all." Or if

it forced you to say to a would-be musician: "Thank you for playing, but you murdered that Etude." Adults' lying is generally altruistic, but children's lying is always local and personal. The best way to make a child a liar for life is to insist that he speak the truth and nothing but the truth. . . .

I have never consciously told a lie to my pupils in thirty-eight years, and indeed never had any desire to. But that is not quite correct, for I told a big lie one term. A girl, whose unhappy history I knew, stole a pound. The theft committee—three boys—saw her spend money on ice cream and cigarettes, and they cross-examined her. "I got the pound from Neill," she told them, and they brought her to me, asking, "Did you give Liz a quid?" Hastily sensing the situation, I replied blandly, "Why, yes, I did." Had I given her away, I knew that forever afterward she would have no trust in me. Her symbolic stealing of love in the form of money would have received another hostile setback. I had to prove that I was on her side all the way. I know that if her home had been honest and free, such a situation would never have arisen. I lied with a purpose—a *curative* purpose—but in all other circumstances, I dare not lie.—A. S. Neill, *Summerhill*

5. That sandwich man I'd replaced had little chance of getting his job back. I went bellowing up and down those train aisles. I sold sandwiches, coffee, candy, cake, and ice cream as fast as the railroad's commissary department could supply them. It didn't take me a week to learn that all you had to do was give white people a show and they'd buy anything you offered them. It was like popping your shoeshine rag. The dining car waiters and Pullman porters knew it too, and they faked their Uncle Tomming to get bigger tips. We were in that world of Negroes who are both servants and psychologists, aware that white people are so obsessed with their own importance that they will pay liberally, even dearly, for the impression of being catered to and entertained

> —Malcolm X, with the assistance of Alex Haley,
> *The Autobiography of Malcolm X*

Sample Approaches and Papers

This section provides, through illustration, some help for students lacking confidence in their ability to *organize* their papers and examination essays.

We provide here five fairly detailed summaries of how competent student writers have approached topics in the subject matter of the social sciences and humanities. We also print in full two of the actual papers. We suggest that you go through the following steps:

1. Look at the topics to be illustrated in this section and think about what is required of the writer.
2. Then read the sample approach and technique sections provided here.
3. Read the example papers, keeping our discussion of the sample approaches in mind.

4. Finally, think about a possible topic in one of your own courses, ideally one that you may (or will) have to face soon, or if you cannot do this, one you have already written about. Try to think out at least two possible approaches to the topic.

1a   QUESTION ABOUT AN ISSUE

Is capital punishment uncivilized?

1b   SAMPLE APPROACH

The writer defended capital punishment. Her unifying idea was:

No, capital punishment is not uncivilized.

Here is how she set about the assignment.

In her first paragraph she claims that capital punishment is a necessary right of a society even if it is not the right of an individual member of the society. She distinguishes between the functions of a society and those of its individual members. Society can force private land to be sold and can draft men for defense, but an individual cannot. These transactions may be necessary to a society. These two examples point up the distinction and show that a society cannot be judged by the same standards as an individual.

In her second paragraph she tries to show that taking human life may be justifiable. First, she says, taking life is not a crime even for an individual if it is done in self-defense. The same rule applies on a larger scale. An army is permitted, even compelled, to kill in order to insure the survival of a society. In both these cases killing is permitted when it means self-defense. The writer is using them as analogies and claiming that capital punishment is essentially the same kind of necessary behavior. Capital punishment is a way society has of defending itself.

In her third paragraph she deals with possible counterarguments. She argues that innocent lives will rarely if ever be taken through capital punishment—and that far more lives will be saved since criminals will be deterred by fear of capital punishment. She provides descriptive detail and a few examples to justify these arguments. So, she concludes, capital punishment is really a civilizing influence since it enables society to take ultimate sanctions against those who violate an essential prohibition.

1c TECHNIQUE

The writer using this approach has really given a three-part answer to the question, or three reasons why she believes that capital punishment is more civilized than uncivilized. The first reason is that capital punishment cannot validly be compared with an individual's killing someone because the state's role differs from that of an individual. The second reason is that capital punishment is the same in some ways as other legitimate ways of killing people. And the third reason is that, far from killing innocent people, capital punishment saves innocent people. (For ways of developing skeletal ideas of this kind, see *Paragraph Development,* particularly the sections on *Cause and Effect, Comparison and Contrast,* pp. 46 and 49.)

2a QUESTION FROM A HISTORY EXAMINATION

The Trade and Navigation Acts were a major factor in provoking the American Revolution. Discuss.

2b SAMPLE APPROACH

This writer shows, in general, that the acts *as a whole* were not a cause of the revolution; only a particular group of them were.

His first paragraph claims that these acts were two very different kinds of legislation—one kind was intended to encourage trade, the other to tax it. The first kind, covering all major acts up to 1763, created strong ties of loyalty. The writer describes benefits such as guaranteed markets, plentiful credit, and efficient transportation. He details the wide support for this legislation in the colonies.

The writer then describes the later laws in some detail, showing that they were passed in Parliament over the opposition of both American and British commercial interests and were intended to benefit only a small Tory clique around the king.

In his last paragraph the writer concludes that these particular laws and their corrupt and ruthless enforcement led to the rapid weakening of American loyalties to Britain and to the justifiable conviction that the British government sought to establish a centralized control over the colonies that would destroy the self-governing powers they had already gained.

2c   TECHNIQUE

The writer using this approach has a three-part essay. The first two parts are a contrast between two different kinds of laws, from which the conclusion, the third part, logically follows. (For ways of developing ideas in these ways, see particularly *Description* and *Comparison and Contrast,* pp. 37 and 49.)

3a   TOPIC GIVEN IN A SOCIOLOGY COURSE

> Choose some significant aspect of modern advertising and discuss its effect on the quality of modern life.

3b   SAMPLE APPROACH

This writer's unifying idea is that certain kinds of American advertising have a powerful impact on women, not only on what they buy but on their sense of identity as well.

She begins with a generalization: Advertisers exploit female insecurity about their femininity. They seek to present domestic life amid plentiful and varied products as the ultimate goal for truly feminine women. (A number of examples.)

In the second paragraph, the writer focusses on the ''help'' that advertising provides a woman in capturing the male who can best satisfy the material hunger the advertising industry has fostered in her. (Examples.)

Paragraph three reveals a related but different kind of manipulation. Advertising seeks to create in inactive women an egotistical self-love that can be satisfied only by indulgence in certain commercial products. (Examples.)

In her conclusion, the writer claims that all such advertising exploits female insecurity and reduces women to objects hungering for commercial products. It seeks to destroy authentic humanness for economic profit.

3c TECHNIQUE

The approach above is essentially an intelligent use of illustrative material to establish and develop generalizations about:

1. what advertisers are doing
2. what effects their actions have
3. what their motives are.

The writer then gives a more generalized statement of the effects and provides a judgment.

3d THE PAPER

Women, Sex, and Advertising

In the last fifty years the psychologists behind the advertising experts have discovered that they can successfully predict the jerks and starts of fashion fads in the American way of life by appealing to the "feminine nature" of housewives, career girls, and teenagers. The sexual sell may take the form of glowing praise for products that "let a woman feel really fulfilled" in her dream home, her all-electric kitchen, her car that is specially designed for a housewife's multiple mobile roles. A woman cannot help but be happy if she is living amidst all the products that vibrate with American domestic wholesomeness and efficiency, and directing family consumption of pure foods, clothing, soaps, toys, and toiletries. The motivating factor in the domestic sexual sell is domestic bliss: a woman should be able to use all her libido in the home and be completely fulfilled as a housewife. Products X, Y, and Z insure that this will happen. Sex at home swings.

Career girls are convinced that they can land the most virile of available playboys if they conscientiously smear their faces with creams and

powders that glow like moonlight, make their skin soft as babies' be-
hinds, and in general give them an irresistible magnetic quality. Not only
cosmetics, but all the objects that a woman wears or surrounds herself
with, should have that "certain indefinable seductiveness" that makes her
world sensual and yielding. Not only must a girl purchase numerous objects for her eventual sexual fulfillment; she must make her very person
into a saleworthy product for show on the "prestige female companion"
market.

(3) Sometimes the sexual sell doesn't connect the woman's desires for
happiness to her relationships with family or lover; rather it lets her "just
be herself." She can dress in soft lingerie and spend hours in bubble
baths or massaging her skin with expensive oils because she owes it to
herself to feel good. Narcissism is an important aspect in the lives of numerous women who do not have a career that they are seriously involved
with, or other social or political work that they consider important. Products that help them feel beautiful and sensually gratified fill an emptiness
that results from an impoverished inner life.

(4) In fact, American advertising, and especially the sexual sell directed
towards women, helps perpetuate a devastating alienation from the self
and from the other. A society built on production and consumption must
make objects out of people in order to convince them that they need an
ever increasing number and variety of products in order to feel fully alive.
The goal is surplus value, or profit. The price is loss of authentic human
relationships—Judy Rosenthal, student

4a ASSIGNMENT GIVEN IN A LITERATURE COURSE

> Choose some aspect of Hemingway's stories that interests you
> and discuss it in relation to two or three of the stories from *In Our
> Time.*

4b SAMPLE APPROACH

This writer decides to focus on Hemingway's own discovery
that

"life is harsh and dull"

She states her unifying idea and lets the reader know that she will
examine two stories from this point of view. Since each story is

accompanied by a "sketch," she will show how this apparently unconnected piece of writing really does have a connection with the overall theme of the story.

Her second paragraph recapitulates the theme of the first story: a young man finding out from a love experience that life is indeed harsh and dull. In the third paragraph the preliminary sketch is also shown to share the same theme.

The fourth and fifth paragraphs provide the same kind of analysis of the second story and sketch. The sketches, she claims, add to or clarify the major themes.

In her final paragraph she summarizes the similarities between two stories. (The view of life presented in them is essentially the same.) Then she ends by contrasting the emphases of the two. One story shows an individual changing in the process of finding out that life is harsh and dull; the other deals with an individual who has made the same discovery but does not change. The story instead gradually reveals more and more about a situation that essentially remains the same.

4c TECHNIQUE

The statement of the writer's unifying idea and direction is followed by illustrations from the two stories. Her concluding paragraph points out the likenesses and differences in Hemingway's treatment of the same basic idea in the two stories.

4d THE PAPER

The Realization of Theme in In Our Time

In Our Time, a collection of short stories connected by brief sketches, seems almost to defy classification. It is not really a novel in any normal sense of the word and although some characters, notably Nick Adams, appear in several stories, none appears in all the stories. Nor is the book simply a collection of unrelated short stories, for the stories, however much they may differ in terms of characters, plot, or setting, do have one unifying element, the verification of Hemingway's "discovery that life is harsh and dull.''[1] None of the stories is tragic and they are perhaps the more powerful because of this: life for most people is not tragic but for many it is certainly harsh and dull. Particularly in those of the stories dealing with young people, the realization of the nature of life (as Hemingway sees it) comes as the result of the clash between the ideal and the real, between what life is supposed to be and what life is. This paper will examine two of the stories which deal with young people, specifically with relation to the way in which the unifying theme of the book is realized both in the stories themselves and by the inclusion of the sketch accompanying each story.

The story ''The End of Something'' really contains two, related endings: the first is the end of a town, the second, the end of a relationship. The old lumbering town of Hortons Bay ceased to exist when the forest had been stripped of its trees and, although every moveable object had been carted off, when Nick and Marjorie pass by ten years later, there is still ''the broken white of its limestone foundations showing through the swampy second growth.''[2] Then, the main part of the story is told; Nick breaks off his relationship with Marjorie, apparently because she ''knows everything,'' and love is not ''fun any more'' (page 40). The ''everything'' that Marjorie knows may be what is indicated by the words of the story––that Nick has taught her all he knows about the outdoors, about fishing and moonrise, and that once he has lost a sort of woodsman's superiority, he finds the relationship intolerable. On the other hand, one can understand Nick's words '''I've taught you everything. You know you do [know everything]''' (page 40) to mean that he has given Marjorie so much of himself and really taught her ''everything'' about himself, that he can no longer feel happy and comfortable with her. Either interpretation seems to be valid. In any event, what is important about the story is that this young man has found that love does not always bring the happiness which one expects from it, and even more important, that this incident will not just fade away. Its pain (its skeleton) will remain to show through the ''second growth'' of Nick's experience as a reminder that life is harsh and dull.

---

[1] Alan Lebowitz, ''Hemingway In Our Time,'' *The Yale Review,* March 1969, V. 58, page 322.

[2] Ernest Hemingway, *In Our Time,* Charles Scribners Sons, New York, 1925, page 36. All remaining quotations in this paper are from this edition.

The brief sketch at the beginning of this story appears to be an allegory for the way young people are equipped to face life. The German soldier who comes over the wall is loaded with all the equipment he has been told he will need to fight the war successfully. When he is shot, he is "awfully surprised" (page 33). And while the story "The End of Something" does not say this is what happened to Nick, the connection is easily made. Nick, and in fact nearly everyone, is loaded down with "equipment" and expectations for life; then when something goes wrong (as it must inevitably in Hemingway's world) and he finds that life and love are not "fun," he is bewildered and hurt.

"Soldier's Home" is the story of a young American soldier's return home after World War I and his realization that whatever he may have done, however brave a man or however good a soldier he was, that reality is not a part of the reality in which he is expected to live the remainder of his life. Had he returned home earlier, when the other soldiers of the town returned, he would have "been welcomed elaborately." However, the story does not lead one to believe that those who returned in time for all the lavish welcomes, hero worship, and hysteria, were in the long run much better off than he. The others did have an audience for their stories and were perhaps able to communicate to others and thereby lessen some of the horror and despair of the war, but soon "the boys are all settling down; they're all determined to get somewhere" (page 99). Krebs does not want to get anywhere. He probably would not have minded being "somewhere" but he was quite unwilling to try to get there. This is indicated quite explicitly with respect to Krebs' feelings about the girls in the town, for they have come to symbolize for him the kind of struggle in which he has no desire to participate again—perhaps because he has realized, however unconsciously, that the results are not what they were advertised to be: He wanted a girl "but they lived in such a complicated world of already defined alliances and shifting feuds that Krebs did not feel the energy or the courage to break into it" (page 92). "He did not want to get into the intrigue and the politics" (page 93). "He did not want any consequences" (page 93). The choice of vocabulary can hardly be accidental; life and love are not at all different from war and Krebs' war appears not to have been tragic, only harsh and dull.

The introductory sketch for this story fits in in much the same manner as the one for "The End of Something." It adds or clarifies a layer of meaning which the reader might otherwise have overlooked. The soldier (probably not Krebs), in a moment of panic, reverts to what was probably one of his original pieces of "equipment"--the belief that there is a God who can really help him out of a dangerous situation. He strikes a bargain to save his life, but after the crisis was over, "he never told anybody" about Jesus (page 87). In addition to the natural reaction anyone might have in similar circumstances--embarrassment at one's own weakness--there seems to be something else at work on the soldier, that is, the realization that "Jesus" is not "the only thing that matters" (page 87). When one is alive on a day that is "hot and muggy and cheerful and quiet" (page 87) nothing matters but that day. Krebs wanted only to have days, isolated days, without plans and without consequences.

(6)   Krebs at the beginning of this story has some of the same general characteristics that Nick Adams has at the end of the story, "The End of Something." Like Krebs, Nick is described in terms of what he <u>doesn't</u> feel, or <u>doesn't</u> do, or <u>doesn't</u> desire. Once experience has come and gone--in the form of love for Nick and war for Krebs--the characters are left with a sense of loss. They are unable and unwilling to join in, to marry or take a job, to anticipate the consequences of their actions, or to see the world, as other men do, in terms of cause and effect. But what I find interesting is that the emphasis is a little different in these two stories. The painful awareness of what the world really is comes to Nick at the end of the story, but it evidently has come to Krebs before the story begins. This makes for an interesting kind of difference: "The End of Something" is about the way a character changes in the course of events, but "Soldier's Home" is not. Krebs doesn't really change; rather the <u>reader's</u> view of him changes and becomes more complete as the story progresses.—Linda Linck, student

Research Papers

In the course of your college work you are likely to have been assigned at least one research paper, resource paper, or library paper. There are two major purposes for such an assignment: (1) to allow for an in-depth study of a narrow topic, and (2) to teach students how to find relevant documents or other resources, how to document source material, and how to write an accurate and balanced account of the findings.

The purpose of this section is to illustrate the format of a research paper. For this reason much of our space is devoted to a sample research paper. Other aspects of the research process are treated very briefly.

Some Basic Rules About Research Papers

1. The topic you choose must interest you; perhaps it should be something that you have already done some reading or thinking about. Your research may confirm half-formed hunches, or it may, of course, undermine them.

2. The topic you choose must make use of your intelligence and judgment. The reader is interested in reading a research paper showing your own considered view of a certain large body of data.

3. As (2) suggests, you must organize your data and findings so that the paper is more than a patchwork of relevant quotations lacking any organizing principle.

4. As a researcher, you must consult an adequate number of sources. If there are far more sources than you have time to read, then you must narrow your topic and thus tell your reader what area you really have covered in depth. (If say, you have consulted only the *Encyclopedia Brittanica,* you should entitle your paper "A Summary of What the *Encyclopedia Brittanica* Says About X"—rather an absurd topic but at least an honest one. Notice how the sample research paper has handled this problem.)

5. You, as the researcher, are responsible for evaluating source material. An astrologer, who tries to interpret the effects of stars and planets on human affairs, is unlikely to be a reliable authority for a serious paper on astronomy. Serious and reputable scholars are generally more reliable than writers for popular magazines, or those who may have vested interests in particular points of view. But judgments of this kind depend in large part on the particular situation.

6. You must not pull source material out of its context in such a way that you distort the original meaning, or present a misleading account because important and relevant material is omitted.

7. In the paper you must give credit to the writers of books and articles that you have consulted. You must use appropriate forms in footnotes and bibliography, forms that will enable any other competent researcher to verify your documentation easily. (See *Footnotes* and *Bibliography* in the sample research paper and pp. 97–102.)

8. Using someone else's words or ideas without footnoting is re-

garded as plagiarism, or dishonesty in the use of source material. Every phrase taken from a book and used in your paper must be placed in quotation marks and footnoted. Every idea taken from a book, even if not directly quoted, must also be footnoted.

9. Do not let the mechanics of footnoting interfere with, or take the place of, the essential business of communicating. Quite often you can give the necessary information in parentheses in the text of the paper, without interrupting the flow of sentences and without the extra baggage of a footnote. (See the *Sample Research Paper* and *How to Footnote.*)

10. The writing should be as clear and interesting as other expository writing. Some writers on very technical subjects include a description of their investigation which can be read without difficulty by the ordinary reader. It is important for all such writers to say in simple language what the research means and, if possible, how it is related to the ordinary man.

Guide to Punctuating Quotations

There are several conventions about the use of quotations and the appropriate way to footnote them.

1. When using your own words to tell what someone has said, do not use quotation marks:

   Alden and Magenis say that slavery was easy to abolish in the North as there were few slaves, but not so easy in the South where the plantation system depended on them.[1]

2. Some quotations are punctuated like conversation in a dialogue. The quoted material is a complete sentence in itself:

   The authors say, ''They had little protection, however, from the occasional vicious owner.''[1]

3. You can combine quoted and unquoted material in one sen-

tence so long as the sentence still reads smoothly and so long as the author's original meaning is not distorted:

> The closest this history comes to describing the slaves themselves is a brief mention that slaves, once working, were seldom cruelly treated ''since it was to the interest of the master to keep them healthy and contented.''[1]

4. Long quotations, three lines or more, should be written as a block, single spaced, and indented four spaces from the left margin. No quotation marks are used. Use a colon to introduce the quotation in most circumstances:

> They describe the typical hardcore slave trader: He is not troubled evidently with a conscience, for although he habitually separates parents from child, brother from sister and husband from wife, he is yet one of the jolliest dogs alive, and never evinces the least sign of remorse. . . .[1]

5. You can use a row of three spaced dots to show that words have been left out (or four dots if one of them represents an omitted period):

> Hamm says ''emancipation involved . . . serious consequences.''[1]

6. You may insert in the quotation clarifying words of your own if you enclose them in brackets:

> Crèvecoeur points out that no one saw the ''hardship of [the slave's] incessant toils.''[1]

The Sample Research Paper

The writer of this sample research paper, a college freshman, chose to investigate the way American high school textbooks had portrayed life as a slave in America. He narrowed the field of investigation by choosing only books published between 1957 and 1971. Of these books he selected ten.

SAMPLE NOTE CARDS

After some preliminary reading in the ten books, the writer began to take notes on 4 x 6 cards. Here are samples of these cards, which illustrate

1. that note cards can contain paraphrases or direct quotations from the source material, as well as the researcher's own conclusions about the information;
2. that the researcher should put quotation marks around every word or phrase taken verbatim from the book;
3. that each card should contain just one bit of information to allow for easy separation and organization of material;
4. that each note card should be labeled with a sub-topic to show what aspect of the topic it concerns (of course, the label might have been added sometime after the note was written, at a time when the writer decided how he was going to organize his material);
5. that only the author's name, possibly an abbreviation of a book title, and page numbers are necessary on the note card;
6. that the information necessary for footnoting is provided by the smaller bibliography card (see sample bibliography card); [Since there are probably many note cards for a single source, the bibliography card will save time since it requires writing this information once instead of several times.]
7. that despite the best of preplanning, some cards have to be thrown away before the actual writing process because they turn out to be redundant or irrelevant.

Compare these cards with the source material and also with the research paper and its outline.

slavery — economic matter

This book seems to be explaining why emancipation was gradual in the South. "But since slaves were more numerous in the South, emancipation involved serious economic and social consequences."

Hamm, p. 270.

Note card 1. This card contains an exact quotation from the source and the student's comment. Note, comparing this with p. 3 of the sample paper, that the student was able to use the material exactly as he wrote it on the card and that he was careful to put quotation marks around what he took verbatim from the book. This helps prevent accidental plagiarism.

A footnote, or other means of crediting, was required in the paper. But since the bibliography card gives the full information necessary for footnoting, the student needed to write on this card only *Hamm* (the author's name) and the page number of the source. (If the writer had been using more than one book by Hamm, he would have had to give the title of the book from which the information came.)

Notice that the phrase at the top of the card, ''slavery—economic matter,'' is a key-in to the outline (Part II-A-1). This card provides evidence for the point the student wanted to make in that part of the paper.

Fragments from Hamm's textbook, *From Colony to World Power.*

p. 270

Compare with Note card 1.

Gradual emancipation in the North. The eighteenth century was a century of enlightenment, in which the doctrine of equality was widely preached. Humanitarian ideas, and the fact that slavery was unprofitable in the North, caused the Northern states, in the last quarter of the eighteenth century, to abolish slavery. Some of the Northern states freed their slaves outright; others provided for gradual emancipation by decreeing that the children born to slave parents should be free.

slavery — treated as a matter affecting politics and legislation

Two long ¶s here. Many details given, describing Lincoln's Emancipation Proclamation and the political effects of it. Show that the Procl. may have won some friends and lost him the support of those who had believed that he was fighting merely to save the Union.

Hamm, p. 342.

Note card 2. This card is keyed in to Part II-A-2 of the outline. Notice that this is a much-shortened paraphrase of the original source material, and notice that the student chooses to focus on only one part of the two-paragraph passage he refers to. (Examine the fragment of the original source.) When he used part of this information in writing the paper, he was required to use a footnote or some other means of crediting, *even though the reference to Hamm's material is brief and there is no direct quotation.*

The emancipation movement in the South. While the Northern states were freeing their slaves, the Southern states were sympathetically discussing the question of emancipation. But since slaves were more numerous in the South, emancipation involved serious economic and social consequences. Nearly all the Southern states had numerous anti-slavery societies. These organizations aided the American Colonization Society, which established the Negro republic of Liberia to which the emancipated American slaves could be transported.

The Emancipation Proclamation. At the time this famous letter was published, Lincoln had already determined upon a course of action, but because the Union forces had met a long series of defeats, he did not think that the time was yet ripe to publish it to the world. In July he told his Cabinet of his intention to issue a proclamation freeing the slaves of the Confederate states, but at

<u>cultural life of the slave is ignored</u>

"The English language, law customs, institutions, and ideals, modified by a new environment and influenced by other European
peoples, were the foundations upon which
the life and culture of the people of the
U.S. were based."
No mention of the base of the life and
culture of the black people of the U.S.

Hamm, p. 25.

Note card 3. This is a note card that was *not used* in the final writing, even though it was a helpful part of the research. (The phrase at the top of the card turned out to be not an aspect of the topic but rather the topic itself.) The words quoted here may have stimulated the student to think of what he wanted to say in the introduction or conclusion of his paper, but he did not use or borrow anyone else's material. Thus no footnote was necessary in the paper.

p. 342

Seward's suggestion he decided to wait until a Northern victory would make the proclamation seem more than empty words. In September, 1862, Lincoln considered Lee's defeat at Antietam an opportune time to announce that if the Confederate states had not laid down their arms by January 1, 1863, their slaves would be free. On January 1 he issued the final proclamation designating the states and parts of the states still controlled by the Confederacy. Since the Proclamation applied only to such territory, it could not immediately effect the freedom of a single slave. It was only a war measure. The Proclamation did not apply to the four slave states—Delaware, Maryland, Kentucky, and Missouri—which had not seceded, nor to those parts of the Confederacy which were already occupied by Northern troops.

Compare with
Note card 2

    Effect of the Proclamation on the purpose of the war. The Emancipation Proclamation made it plain to all that the war meant much more than the preservation of the Union and the exclusion of slaves from the federal territories. If the North were victorious, it would mean a new nation without slavery. Whether the Proclamation made more friends for the President in the United States than it cost him is hard to say. Lincoln had repeatedly stated that the war would go on until the Union was safe. Now he seemed to say that it would go on until the slaves were free. A popular bit of verse widely used by the Democrats in the Congressional campaign of 1862 stated:

> Honest Old Abe, when the war first began
> Denied abolition was part of his plan;
> Honest Old Abe has since made a decree,
> The war must go on till the slaves all are free.
> As both can't be honest, will someone tell how,
> If Honest Abe then, he is Honest Abe now?

It is impossible to say whether the losses sustained by the Republican party in the mid-term elections of 1862 were due to dislike for the Emancipation Proclamation or whether the Proclamation saved the party from complete defeat.

The transplanting of English institutions. The colonization of America meant the spread into a savage land of European modes of living, languages, ideals of life. In the Spanish and Portuguese colonies it meant a mingling with the natives, forming sometimes, as in Mexico and Brazil, a settlement practically native in appearance. In the English colonies, however, this was not the case, for wherever the English settled, they crowded the red men back into the interior. As a result, English civilization, as it spread into the American wilderness, remained predominantly English. The English language, law, customs, institutions, and ideals, modified by a new environment and influenced by other European peoples, were the foundations upon which the life and culture of the people of the United States were based.

p. 25

Compare with Note card 3.

SAMPLE BIBLIOGRAPHY CARD

The bibliography card contains three kinds of information: the author, the title, and publication information—the place of publication, the publishing company, and the date. It is also convenient to list the library call number—in case the researcher wants to find the book for a second time—but this number does not go into the actual bibliography. At the time of typing the bibliography, the writer alphabetizes the cards by last name of the author and checks a sample bibliography for proper format.

> Hamm, William A. *From Colony to
> World Power: A History of the United States*
> Lexington, Mass.: D. C. Heath, 1957.

Note card 4. In this case there was no library call number.

(See *The Bibliography*, p. 101, for ways of dealing with periodicals, anthologies, and so forth.)

AN ANALYSIS OF THE TREATMENT OF SLAVERY

IN SELECTED HIGH SCHOOL TEXTBOOKS

Alan Phillips
English Composition

An Analysis of the Treatment of Slavery

in Selected High School Textbooks

SENTENCE OUTLINE

This is the
writer's unifying
statement.

Thesis: Generally high school history textbooks discuss slavery only
as it affected the white man with little or no mention of
Negroes as people; better understanding of the black American
today could be achieved by expanding texts to include this
large minority.

Introduction

I. This paper demonstrates how little information there is in a
selected number of high school history textbooks about the history
of the black American.

II. For generations American history has been taught as it affected
the white man, excluding almost completely the effect the history
of the American Negro had on the developing states and on today's
society.

A. This is especially true of the earlier textbooks which, in
general, cover only these areas:

1. slavery and the economy

2. laws about slavery

3. the abolition movement

B. These texts generally communicate the myth of the "happy"
slave.

1. They ignore the high mortality rate among slaves, the
human rights denied Africans, the treatment of slaves on
board ship and on the plantation, and what it was like to
be a slave.

2. They point out the "positive" aspects of slavery.

3. Two texts, Planer-Neff and Wyman-Ridge, are possible
exceptions.

4. But none of these texts give the kind of description that
Crèvecoeur gave his book published in 1782.

Outline - 2

III. The books examined of later publication date describe more objec-
tively the role of the Negro in the development of the United
States, but coverage still pertains mainly to the Negro as he
affects the white man.

    A. The text published in 1966, although dealing largely with the
economic effects of slavery, does cover some of the evils of
the slave trade and the Negroes' organized revolts.

    B. The text published in 1969 has an even more contemporary
approach toward the inclusion of the Negro in United States
history.

        1. It gives descriptions of the civilized communities in
West Africa.

        2. It provides details on the high mortality rate and the
low life expectancy on sugar plantations.

        3. There is also some attempt to describe the living and
working conditions of the slaves.

        4. This text mentions the punishments for runaway Negroes
and gives reasons for the white man's fear of the free
black man.

    C. The last and most recent publication in 1970 shows pronounced
changes in the treatment of Negroes by history textbooks.

        1. The description of the economic effects of slavery brings
to light the false conceptions of the state of slavery in
older textbooks.

        2. Included are comparative accounts of slave life by an
English aristocrat and by an ex-slave.

IV. Good as they are, these modern books still fail to include dis-
cussions of much of what made up the life of the Negro slave.

V. History textbooks could be expanded to include more on the background of the Negro and would thus better educate every American
on the history of the United States, whatever his race.

Concluding
paragraphs

An Analysis of the Treatment of Slavery

in Selected High School Textbooks

Part I introduces the idea that history textbooks for high school students should portray the lives of black as well as white Americans. It poses the central question: have they done so?

[The writer footnoted this information because she found slightly different figures in different sources. The discrepancy was not important enough to comment on, however.]

    Every year at Thanksgiving the exploits of some white men who landed in Massachusetts more than three centuries back are celebrated with considerable ceremony. Children have learned about them in history lessons for more than two centuries, for these Pilgrims are thought of as in some sense not just the founders of this nation but also as the ancestors of the American people today. Children have learned in school about the way the early white settlers lived, about the way Southern Belles entertained in their Southern mansions and about how rumbustious cowboys conquered the West, cowboys even now thought of as pure Caucasian. But approximately one in every eight Americans is black.[1]

    How much have children learned about the ways of that American's ancestors? And is the situation changing? If understanding the history of this country is necessary for understanding American civilization today, then an almost complete ignorance of the past of a large segment of the population would hardly be an asset for understanding the thoughts and feelings of black Americans, or for black Americans to understand their own situation. Since the schools are the major instruments for passing on knowledge of the country's past, the books used in the school, particularly of course the history texts, should provide some answers to the questions posed above.

-2-

The textbooks discussed in this paper cover a period of thirteen years. The earliest book examined was published three years after the Supreme Court decision on the Brown vs. Board of Education of Topeka case (1954), which sparked a powerful civil rights movement and decreed that segregation had no place in the education system.[2]

The first section of books to be discussed were published between 1957 and 1964.

> 1957--Hamm, <u>From Colony to World Power</u>
> 1958--Bragdon and McCutchen, <u>History of a Free People</u>
> 1961--Craven and Johnson, <u>American History</u>
> 1962--Alden and Magenis, <u>A History of the United States</u>
> 1962--Planer and Neff, <u>Freedom Under Law</u>
> 1963--Steinberg, <u>The United States--Story of a Free People</u>
> 1964--Wyman and Ridge, <u>The American Adventure</u>

In these books the discussion of slaves and slavery up to the time of the Civil War is limited to the economic advantages of slavery, the legislation regarding the institution of slave labor, and the abolition movement.

The first mention of slavery in the Craven and Johnson book is in connection with the growth of agriculture; farms gave way to plantations, and "the number of servants and slaves in kitchens and fields grew."[3] These authors, as well as Steinberg, and Planer and Neff, all emphasize that slaves were a necessity in the cotton industry especially after the introduction of the cotton gin.[4] In the text written by Bragdon and McCutchen, the Negroes are seen as a sign of prosperity of Southern society rather than people in their own right (Steinberg, pp. 269-271). Although they show that some plantation owners deplored the system of slavery, still their most detailed explanations are concerned with how difficult it was for the white

Part II in the original is seven to eight pages long. It gives a "no" answer to the question raised in the introduction-- i.e., "No, these books do not adequately portray the lives of black Americans." The purpose of this section is to show in what way this statement is true and to what extent it is true.

[Part of this sentence is paraphrase. The writer has not quoted directly but has used the idea of another, and thus a footnote was necessary. The original words were written by Earl Warren and quoted by S. E. Morison: "We conclude that in the field of public education the doctrine of 'separate but equal' has no place."]

Part II, A

This comes from Note card 1.

-3-

man, in an economic sense, to free the slaves.[5] Hamm, for example, says, "since slaves were more numerous in the South, emancipation involved serious economic and social consequences."[6]

[The student then details the textbooks' coverage of laws regarding slavery and the abolition movement. After this he begins B of Part II, ''the myth of the happy slave,'' of which we print a portion below.]

-8-

    Other books in this group try to balance the negative aspects of being a slave with its "positive" aspects. Alden and Magenis, while they mention that slaves lived in huts, also state that they had gardens in which to cultivate food. They say that some slaves "learned to read and write" (p. 198). Naturally they do not fail to mention the inevitable "many planters who treated their slaves well," and the fact that Andrew Jackson was fond of his slaves and always spoke of them as "the family." They point out that a very few masters were cruel but otherwise imply that slaves were generally happy. Yet at the same time they say, "Sometimes slaves tried to escape, and many owners lived in fear of slave revolt" (p. 198). This appears to contradict the earlier implication of the authors that most slaves were happy and contented.

    Planer and Neff give more detail on the topic of escape. They note that even the possibility of it was denied by the passing of the fugitive slave law, which provided heavy penalties for helping fugitives escape. But while their discussion is sympathetic in tone, they give few details to show what it was to be a slave.

Part II, B

Part II, B

-9-

The most recent book in this category, Wyman and Ridge's The American Adventure, says more about the actual working conditions of slaves. It describes the old stereotypes of slave life--the slaves going happily about their work singing gaily in the fields--and emphasizes that the stereotypes are false (p. 254). There are fairly full descriptions of the selling of slaves. This text is the only one to report that family units had been broken up. The book quotes a contemporary account of the typical hardcore slave trader (p. 260):[10]

> He is not troubled evidently with a conscience,
> for although he habitually separates parents
> from child, brother from sister and husband from
> wife, he is yet one of the jolliest dogs alive,
> and never evinces the least sign of remorse . . .

Crèvecoeur had said much the same thing (p. 156): "The daughter torn from her weeping mother, the child from the wretched parents, the wife from the loving husband . . ."

Of the authors mentioned, Crèvecoeur alone emphasizes the pitiful position of the black people. Even though they might have Sundays off, they were obliged to look after their own bits of land to feed themselves and their families. Many slaves had nothing to make up for their miseries, neither good food nor kindness, but only fear of the whip and death (pp. 159-160).

> . . . they are obliged to devote their lives,
> their limbs, their will, and every vital exertion
> to swell the wealth of the masters; who look not
> upon them with half the kindness and affection
> with which they consider their dogs and horses. (p. 156)

The second category of books to be discussed, those of more recent publication, contains titles published in 1966, 1969, and 1970, respectively.

Here the writer begins Part III of the paper. He demonstrates that the newer

books give more
coverage to the
history of black
Americans. As in
Part II, he shows
in what way this
is true and to
what extent.

-10-

```
1966--Link and Muzzey, Our American Republic
1969--Bartlett and others, A New History of the United States
1970--Freidel and Drewry, America--A Modern History of the
      United States
```

These histories illustrate the more modern trends towards

recognizing for the black a more important role in the development

of the United States than that of a possession, economic entity, or

Part III   instrument of the white man's progress. However, they still tend to

allocate far greater coverage to the economic advantages of the slave

and to the abolition movement than to the slave himself, his living

and working conditions, and his family life--where it existed.

-13-

A typical example of the remarkable change in modern textbooks

is Freidel and Drewry's A Modern History of the United States,

published in 1970.[13] This text describes the economic effects of

slavery on Southern society in a manner which points out to the

reader the possible flaws in older textbooks. The authors say, for

Part III, C   example, "The plantation owners sometimes convinced outsiders that

they were indeed the benefactors of the slaves" (p. 253). There is

a detailed account by an African kidnapped from his native land,

where he was a member of an aristocratic family. He describes in his

own words conditions on the boat and finally his sale as a slave.

This man, Olaudah Equiano, was fortunate in his purchaser. He became

educated and finally a free man, and thus able to write about his

-14-

adventures (p. 25). The book also provides two different perspectives on plantation slave life, which should give the student a fair idea of how the picture of living conditions can be distorted. One is a description by Sir Charles Lyell, an English geologist and aristocrat, and a guest of the plantation owner. The second is an account written by an ex-slave, Solomon Northrup, who himself experiences life as a slave on this same plantation (pp. 254-255). This marked contrast reveals that most textbook historians in the past had a tendency to ignore the slave's side of the story and to choose descriptions biased in favor of the white man's view of slavery.

> Part III, C

Good as they are, these more modern books still fail to include much of what made up the life of the Negro either as a slave or as a free man. There is nothing to imply that any form of African culture was brought with them, yet these Africans obviously must have held on to certain traditions which may have influenced the modern generations of black people.

> This corresponds to Part IV of the outline, though it could have been part of III or the beginning of V.

A reasonable understanding of this black background could better be achieved if the history textbooks were expanded to describe the black music, the black family units, the folk tales and other cultural traditions which the blacks still held onto either as slaves or as free men. Such knowledge should form part of every American's educational background, whatever his race. He should not have to wait for a college course in "Black Studies."

> This is the concluding ¶, or Part V of the outline.

[The writer used footnotes only for the <u>first</u> reference to a source. For all subsequent references he used parentheses in the body of the paper. Thus the reader did not have to interrupt his reading more than necessary. Giving the publisher and place of publication is permissible but not absolutely necessary since this information is included in the Bibliography.]

-15-

FOOTNOTES

[1] Stephen J. Wright, "The Status of the Negro in America." in <u>The World Almanac, 1971</u>, ed. Luham H. Long (New York: World Almanac, 1970), p. 45.

[2] Samuel Eliot Morison, <u>The Oxford History of the American People</u> (New York: Oxford University Press, 1965), p. 1086.

[3] Avery O. Craven and Walter Johnson, <u>American History</u> (Lexington, Mass.: Ginn, 1961), p. 41.

[4] See Craven and Johnson, pp. 228-229; Mabel G. Planer and William L. Neff, <u>Freedom Under Law</u> (Milwaukee: Bruce Publishing Company, 1962), p. 240; Samuel Steinberg, <u>The United States--Story of a Free People</u> (Boston: Allyn and Bacon, 1963), p. 228.

[5] Henry W. Bragdon and Samuel P. McCutchen, <u>History of a Free People</u> (New York: Macmillan, 1958), p. 64.

[6] William A. Hamm, <u>From Colony to World Power</u> (Lexington, Mass.: D. C. Heath, 1957), p. 270.

[7] John R. Alden and Alice Magenis, <u>A History of the United States</u> (New York: American Book Company, 1962), p. 85.

[8] Walker D. Wyman and Martin Ridge, <u>The American Adventure</u> (Chicago: Lyons and Carnahan, 1964), p. 258.

[9] Michel-Guillaume Jean de Crèvecoeur, <u>Letters from an American Farmer</u> (1782; rpt. New York: E. P. Dutton, 1957), p. 155.

[10] The original source for this quotation is not given.

[11] Arthur S. Link and David S. Muzzey, <u>Our American Republic</u> (Lexington, Mass.: Ginn, 1966), p. 48.

[12] Irving Bartlett, et al., <u>A New History of the United States</u> (New York: Holt Rinehart and Winston, 1969), p. 35.

[13] Frank Freidel and Henry N. Drewry, <u>America--A Modern History of the United States</u> (Lexington, Mass.: D. C. Heath, 1957), p. 253.

-16-

BIBLIOGRAPHY

Alden, John R., and Alice Magenis. A History of the United States.
    New York: American Book Company, 1962.

Bartlett, Irving, Edwin Fenton, David Fowler and Seymour Mandelbaum.
    A New History of the United States. New York: Holt Rinehart
    and Winston, 1969.

Bragdon, Henry W., and Samuel P. McCutchen. History of a Free People.
    New York: Macmillan, 1958.

Craven, Avery O., and Walter Johnson. American History. Lexington,
    Mass.: Ginn, 1961.

de Crèvecoeur, Michel-Guillaume Jean. Letters from an American
    Farmer. 1782; rpt. New York: E. P. Dutton, 1957.

Freidel, Frank, and Henry N. Drewry. America--A Modern History of the
    United States. Lexington, Mass.: D. C. Heath, 1970.

Hamm, William A. From Colony to World Power. Lexington, Mass.:
    D. C. Heath, 1957.

Link, Arthur S., and David S. Muzzey. Our American Republic.
    Lexington, Mass.: Ginn, 1966.

Long, Luman H., ed. The World Almanac, 1971. New York: Newspaper
    Enterprise Association, Inc., 1970.

Morison, Samuel Eliot. The Oxford History of the American People.
    New York: Oxford University Press, 1965.

Planer, Mabel G., and William L. Neff. Freedom Under Law.
    Milwaukee: Bruce Publishing Company, 1962.

Steinberg, Samuel. The United States--Story of a Free People.
    Boston: Allyn and Bacon, 1963.

Todd, Lewis P., and Merle Curti. Rise of the American Nation.
    New York: Harcourt Brace Jovanovich, 1961.

Wyman, Walker D., and Martin Ridge. The American Adventure.
    Chicago: Lyons and Carnahan, 1964.

This paper reveals careful consideration of a complex and interesting topic. It is well organized; your own conclusions are clearly stated, carefully documented. Narrowing your topic to a few textbooks was a good thing to do since the narrowing cut down on the amount of material you assumed responsibility for. You should probably have given the criteria for selecting <u>these</u> ten rather than another ten. This is because there is always the possibility that these ten are quite different from the group as a whole. If you chose the books simply because they were the only ones you found in the library, then you should probably have said so. If these ten were the only ones in wide use over the country during the time period you mention, then that fact would have made your paper even more persuasive. Your writing on the whole is clear and interesting, and I think it would interest a large audience.

Footnotes

WHEN TO FOOTNOTE OR GIVE CREDIT TO A SOURCE

Footnotes indicate the precise source of your information. They allow the interested reader to verify the information and find out more detail.

1. Source material is often simply background reading done by the researcher. As such it will not appear in the footnotes, but it may appear in the bibliography.
2. Sometimes the writer uses an idea suggested to him by a particular passage in a book or magazine, by something he has read in the course of the investigation. This idea should be footnoted. (Sometimes people doing scholarly or scientific writing will even footnote ideas given to them by friends in conversation.)
3. If an idea or a fact is *not* new or original—or if it is something the researcher read quite a long time ago and he has since read it in other places—then it is part of a general pool of knowledge or ideas; it really does not belong to anyone in particular. Such ideas are *not* footnoted. For example, one would not footnote the fact that the Great Wall of China was 1500 miles long if he was fairly sure that this was an undisputed piece of information. He would, however, footnote such information if he had found another source saying the Wall was 1800 miles long. The footnote would be used for pointing out the discrepancy. Information about how an abacus works or what a sea anemone eats would not be footnoted because such information is generally available from many sources including major encyclopedias.
4. The writer can paraphrase, or put into his own words, material from books and magazines. In this case footnoting is necessary. (Note paraphrases in the Sample Research Paper. These were used instead of direct quotations to make for smoother, easier reading.)

5. Many items can be credited without a footnote. Use parentheses in cases where the inserted material does not seriously impede the reader. The Sample Research Paper was able to omit nearly thirty footnotes in this way.

HOW TO FOOTNOTE

Footnotes give readers all the information they would need for finding the original sources:

name of the author in full
name of the work
name of the magazine or anthology it appears in, if necessary, and
its volume or series number
name of the editor or translator
name of the publishing company (necessary for ordering a book)
date of publication (to let the reader know when the work was
written, as well as to indicate whether or not it might still be in
print. Include the date of *original* publication as well as the date
of the reprint you may be using.)

TYPING. Recent style manuals suggest typing all footnotes at the end of the paper. Single-space all lines of the footnote and double-space between the notes. Indent the first line five spaces, type the footnote number slightly above the line, and skip a space before the first word. Type the note as you would a sentence, using a capital letter at the beginning, a period at the end, commas and parentheses for separation of the various parts. Type the name of the author in normal order, first name first. (Study the *Sample Footnotes.*)

Footnotes may, alternatively, be typed at the bottom of the page. If so, they are single-spaced with a double space between the notes. These footnotes should be numbered consecutively, not by pages, to avoid confusion in typing the paper or having it printed.

SECOND REFERENCES.   Your first reference to a source should be fully footnoted, but later references can be given credit in a simpler way. A second reference to a play by Shakespeare or a book by Isaac Asimov might be given in parentheses in the body of the paper:

(*Romeo and Juliet,* Act III)

(3. 2. 22–24) or (III, ii, 22–24)   to show the act, scene, and
                                           lines of a play

(Asimov, p. 413)
(Asimov, *Guide,* p. 413)   to show the distinction, say,
                                           between two books by Asimov,
                                           both referred to in your paper

Inserting second references into the body of the paper, as recommended by the *Style Sheet* of the Modern Language Association, saves the reader the trouble of looking for footnotes more often than is necessary. Second references can be given in brief footnotes, instead of parentheses, especially if these footnotes appear at the bottom of the page rather than at the end of the paper.

[1] Asimov, p. 413.

[2] Reeves, p. 92.

[3] Miller, *Psychology,* p. 3.   to differentiate from another work
                                       by Miller referred to in your paper

Some writers still use *ibid.,* meaning ''the same source as cited in the last footnote,'' or *op. cit.,* meaning ''in the work already cited, though not necessarily in the footnote just before this one.'' But in your own writing it is best to avoid the Latin phrases, since they are more difficult than English for most people to understand.

SAMPLE FOOTNOTES

Book with one author	[1] Felix Greene, *Let There Be a World* (Palo Alto, California; Fulton Publishing, 1963), p. 62.
Book with two authors	[2] Stephen Toulmin and June Goodfield, *The Fabric of the Heavens* (New York: Harper & Row, 1961), p. 33.
Book with more than one relevant date	[3] Michel-Guillaume Jean de Crèvecoeur, *Letters from an American Farmer* (1782; rpt. New York: E. P. Dutton, 1957), p. 155.
Book with a translator or editor	[4] Schoolboys of Barbiana, *Letter to a Teacher,* trans. Nora Rossi and Tom Cole (New York: Random House, Vintage Books, 1971), p. 154.
Short work in a collection	[5] Ronald Gross, "Now It's Pepsi," *Pop Poems* (New York: Simon and Schuster, 1967), p. 15.
Newspaper editorial or article with a byline	[6] James J. Kilpatrick, "Public Employees, Unions, and the Right to Work," *Los Angeles Times,* 20 March 1972, Part II, p. 7, Col. 5.
Newspaper article without author	[7] "Navy Pulls Out Secret Porpoise Team That Guarded Viet Harbor," (UPI news service, dateline Saigon) *Los Angeles Times,* 19 March 1972, p. 1, col. 5. [When the author is unnamed, it is useful to name the news service.]
Magazine article without author	[8] "What Price Disney World?" *Consumer Reports,* March 1972, p. 173. [This magazine has a volume number and an issue number, but the date is sufficient for a magazine so readily available in most libraries. No comma is needed when a question mark already divides one element from the next.]
Article with volume number	[9] Randall H. Waldron, "The Naked, The Dead, and The Machine: A New Look at Norman Mailer's First Novel," *PMLA,* 87

(March 1972), 272.

[*PMLA* stands for *Publications of the Modern Language Association,* a journal published every month. This article appears in Volume 87 on p. 272 of the March 1972 issue. The volume number is given directly after the title in Arabic numerals (5 rather than V) and without the abbreviation vol. or v. The date, when it follows a volume number, is enclosed in parentheses and page numbers are written without p. or pp.]

The Bibliography

The bibliography provides in one convenient place a list of the materials used by the writer. It includes all the publication details necessary to anyone looking for the book, magazine, or recording. The publisher's name is included primarily to help anyone wishing to buy a copy.

You should type items in alphabetical order by the last name of the author. Indent the second, third, and fourth lines to make the author's name in the first line stand out. Double-space every line and leave a double space between entries. Include all subtitles and the complete names of authors. Punctuate by separating with periods the three main divisions: author, title, and publishing information.

Article with anonymous author	Anon. "Navy Pulls Out Secret Porpoise Team That Guarded Viet Harbor." UPI news service, *Los Angeles Times,* 19 March 1972, p. 1, col. 5.
Book with more than one relevant date	de Crèvecoeur, Michel-Guillaume Jean. *Letters From an American Farmer.* 1782; rpt. New York: E. P. Dutton, 1957.
Book with one author	Greene, Felix. *Let There Be a World.* Palo Alto, California: Fulton Publishing, 1963.

Book with two
authors

Jacobs, Roderick A., and Peter S. Rosenbaum.
Transformations, Style, and Meaning. Lexington, Mass.: Xerox College Publishing, 1971.
[The name of the second author is typed in normal order, first name first.]

Short work in
a collection

Nash, Ogden. "The Sniffle" in *Poems to
Enjoy,* ed. Dorothy Petitt. London: Macmillan,
1967, p. 24.

Book with translator or
editor

Schoolboys of Barbiana. *Letter to a Teacher,*
trans. Nora Rossi and Tom Cole. New York:
Random House, Vintage Books, 1971.

Article with
volume number

Waldron, Randall H. "The Naked, the Dead,
and the Machine: A New Look at Norman
Mailer's First Novel." *PMLA,* 87 (March
1972), 271–277.

[Volume numbers, like 87 above, are written
without the abbreviations vol. or v. Following
a volume number, dates are enclosed in parentheses and page numbers are written without
the letters pp. or p.]

Standard References in the Library

Guide to Reference Books by Constance M. Winchell

This is an index of indexes, or one large book which will tell
you the names of dictionaries, bibliographies, and other indexes.
This entry on electronic music, for example, tells where to find an
extended list of books on the topic. All abbreviations are explained
in the front of the reference.

The Humanities | Music

Electronic music

Cross, Lowell M., comp. A bibliography of electronic
music. [Toronto], Univ. of Toronto Pr., [1967]. 126pp. $5.
67–2573.   **2BH25**

More than 1,500 entries; author listing with subject index.
Rev.: *CH* 4:636.

Davies, Hugh. Répertoire international des musiques électroacoustiques. International electronic music catalog. Cambridge, Mass., distr. by M.I.T. Pr., [1968]. 330pp. $10. 68–20151. **2BH26**
Intends as far as possible "to document all the electronic music ever composed in the almost twenty years since composers first began to work in this medium."—*Compiler's Pref.* Listing is by country, then by city and studio:

The Encyclopedia Brittanica

This is a helpful start for many topics. Consult the bibliography at the end of the article.

The Reader's Guide to Periodical Literature

Look up authors, subjects of any kind, or titles of articles which you believe may be included in magazines from the present back to 1890. (Another guide, *Poole's Index,* will take you back even further.)

The Social Sciences and Humanities Index

Consult this index for material likely to appear in more scholarly journals.

A special paperback guide that you might want to purchase is *Reference Books: How to Select and Use Them* by Saul Galin and Peter Spielberg, Vintage Book V–561. This guide also has helpful hints on library research and documentation.

Suggested Topics

The following suggestions may help you find a topic that you would like to pursue. Almost all of them are much too broad and would have to be narrowed according to your interests and the material available.

African tribes and the growth of nationalism

Alphabets

The American Revolution from the point of view of the English
Parliament and King

Animals: the recent history of a particular species of animal—
involving the conflict of human interests (for example, the deer,
otter, seal, snail, prairie dog, eagle, leopard)

Children's games, learned from peers and passed from generation
to generation

Children's language

China: the role of Chiang Kai-shek in the development of modern
China

Creation of the solar system: rival theories

Dams: the Aswan Dam

Dams: controversies over the U.S. Corps of Engineers

Disarmament conferences

Earthquakes in America

Energy: disagreements over the ''energy crisis''

Farming: the small farm

Free schools

Guatemala: contemporary events in Guatemala (or another small
Central or South American country)

Hemingway, from the point of view of other writers and artists

Human Behavior: human control of human behavior

Instruction for bilingual children

Jazz in the 30's, as contrasted with jazz in another time period

Job prospects for graduating seniors

Justice: poor people and the courts

Language and aphasia

Language and thought (To what extent does language determine
what we think?)

Martian canals

Medical care: differing approaches to medical care in England,
Sweden, Japan, the U.S.

Music: two kinds of music or two kinds of instruments

Picasso: late work and early work (or the work of another artist)

Poets: comparison of the subject matter of three or four contemporary poets

Pollution of Lake Erie (or another body of water)

Pollution: public attitudes toward pollution in the last ten years

The Presidency: public attitudes toward any past U.S. president during his office

Science and moral responsibility (in a particular context)

Strikes: attitudes toward strikes as a negotiating tool

Students and police

Students and the public

Textbooks: attitudes toward a particular minority in selected history textbooks

Textbooks: presentation of another country (countries) in elementary geography books

TV and education: How effective is TV?

TV: freedom of the press and network TV

The Vitamin C controversy

War: public attitudes at the time toward the War of 1812 and the Spanish-American War

Women: their role in selected children's stories

A Writer's Grammar

Grammar and Syntax

A grammar of a language is a description of how the FORMS of a language—sentences, phrases, words, sounds—are matched to the MEANINGS expressed. For the writer, the most useful part of a grammar is likely to be SYNTAX, the rules we follow, usually unconsciously, when we form sentences. Break these rules and the result will not only be ungrammatical, but also, sometimes, an incoherent string of words:

> What architecture is if you disregard the technical points of designing buildings and town planning, and then you must concern yourself with creating environments for every scale of human association.

However, merely following the syntactic rules does not necessarily guarantee that you have found the best way to express your

107

meaning. The full meaning of a sentence depends on the meanings of each word and also on the ways the words are arranged and grouped together in a sentence. Different groupings are likely to result in different emphases, even though the basic meanings are the same. The following sentence

> Creating environments for every scale of human association must be the concern of architects, rather than just designing buildings or planning towns.

is a good one. It has the same basic meaning as this sentence:

> Architects must be concerned not just with building design or town planning but with the creation of environments for every scale of human association.

But the second version places more emphasis on the role of architects by mentioning them at the very beginning. At the same time, the important final position is used for ''The creation of environments . . .'' While the first sentence ends a little flatly, the second builds up to a climax. Try saying them aloud. You as a writer have to arrange forms in the way that seems to express most accurately and clearly what you want to say. If you are not already an accomplished writer, an awareness of English sentence structure may be quite useful. But first you must be aware of one fact: any language is really a set of dialects.

Dialects and Speech

Each speaker of English speaks it in a slightly different way. But certain general characteristics of pronunciation, vocabulary, and syntax mark off groups of speakers as belonging to a certain location, class, age group, or other kind of speech community. The language of each of these groups is known as a dialect. Differing degrees of social prestige are assigned to these groups of dialects. Certain vowel sounds or sentence formation are often regarded as "pure," "correct," "educated," or "standard," while others are condemned as "impure," "incorrect," "ignorant," "substandard" (or more charitably, "nonstandard"). In England a native speaker who fails to pronounce the *h* in "herb" may be labeled "uneducated" though, of course, he must omit the *h* sound for "honest." Such a valuation arises from economic and psychological stresses in a society rather than any sound linguistic criteria. In that speaker's dialect dropping *h* is a general and logical rule. Similarly speakers, both black and white, of some American dialects don't pronounce the final *t* in words like "accept" or "insist." But although such speakers may follow this pronunciation rule rigorously, they are still apt to be told by speakers of more prestigious dialects that their English is "incorrect."

A writer should be aware of the fact of dialect and its systematic nature so that he can understand his own dialect system and those of others without superior or inferior feelings. Speakers of one dialect should not be forced into substituting other dialect forms merely to satisfy social pressures from the influential.

Written Dialects

Although some dialect differences are carried over from spoken English to written English and even, in the case of Black English, used as the basis for a written literary language, no one's written English is the same as his spoken English. Say aloud the sentences of this paragraph and you will be very conscious of how hard it would be to make them sound like part of a natural conversation. An examination of newspaper articles, scientific reports, student papers, personal letters, and automobile warranties will soon show that written English varies more according to the conventions or "style" expected for each such activity and the readers to whom the writing is addressed. Written English is learned later in life than spoken language and is acquired with more difficulty.

Grammaticality and Correctness

All dialects of English, written or spoken, share certain ways of arranging subjects and objects, prepositions and nouns, and the like. They have a common vocabulary of English words whose meanings remain for the most part constant for all dialects, especially the written ones. Certain grammatical restrictions arise from some meanings. Whether you are writing in London, England, or Jackson, Mississippi, or Wellington, New Zealand, you must still obey such restrictions as the following if your writing is to be recognized as a normal and comprehensible sample of English prose:

1. The verbs "hope," "hate," and "admire" cannot have the noun "walls" as their LOGICAL subject, i.e., walls cannot hope, hate, or admire except in works of fantasy. It is, however, possible to make "walls" the GRAMMATICAL subject for verbs like these:

   Walls are hated and abominated by prisoners and children.

   Here, as in all passive sentences, the LOGICAL subject ("prisoners and children") is not the GRAMMATICAL subject. However, for almost every such passive sentence there is an active one with basically the same meaning, for example,

   Prisoners and children hate and abominate walls.

2. The verb "elapse" cannot have an object.
3. The phrase "on account of" cannot be followed immediately by the verb "sings."

Breaking rules like these will result in incorrect sentences in any English dialect (except for certain kinds of experimental English found in some literary works). For instance, the following sentences collected from real speakers and writers are wrong in a similar way, though less obviously so, and they would be wrong in any dialect.

   I really want to impart upon you just how big our used car sale is.

(The speaker probably meant ''impress'' rather than ''impart.'' ''Impart'' requires different prepositions and objects after it.)

> War is the lesser of two evils. It will inhabit the earth as long as man does.

(Man can inhabit the earth, but war cannot inhabit anything. The logical subject of ''inhabit'' has to be an animate noun, one referring to people or animals.)

> There I was, standing in front of a crowd of people in this sparse turquoise negligee.

(A negligee can be thin, transparent, or polka-dotted, but it cannot be ''sparse.'' Only collective nouns like ''population'' and ''vegetation,'' which refer to something that can be broken up and scattered around, can be sparse.)

EXERCISE

The explanations in parentheses above are statements about rules of English. Make similar statements about the sentences below, explaining what rules have been violated. This is to help you grasp what a *rule* is.

1. The administration's intervention deteriorated the situation gravely.
2. So remembered was the Cid that his story was written fifty years after his death.
3. It is advisable that the mines will be closed down immediately.
4. He sailed to the west coast of Africa with the hope to reach India.
5. The Romans however avoided to cross the Rhine.

Basic Meaning and Surface Meaning

There are many ways of telling the same joke, but they are not all equally funny. Similarly there may be many sentences which appear to have the same meaning:

(1) Public criticism inspired the senator to vote against the canal project.

(2) The senator was inspired by public criticism to vote against the canal project.

(3) What inspired the senator to vote against the canal project was public criticism.

(4) It was the senator who was inspired by public criticism to vote against the canal project.

But they do not have exactly the same meaning. That is, they are not completely synonymous. However, in every case the senator votes against something, that something is always the canal project, and the inspiration for the vote is always public criticism. The BASIC MEANING—who does what because of what—is the same. Such a basic meaning is sometimes called the DEEP STRUCTURE of the sentence. All four sentences share the same deep structure; they are basically synonymous. But the words are not arranged in the same ways—the grammatical subjects are different, and so on—and so they are said to have a different SURFACE STRUCTURE. This difference in surface structure adds an extra dimension of meaning which may be called SURFACE MEANING. In spoken English a speaker may vary his stress, rhythm, or voice pitch to adjust the surface meaning still further. However, we shall concern ourselves here with written English.

Contrast the first and third sentences. The third differs in surface meaning in that it seems to assume or presuppose that the reader already knows what the senator did. It communicates the new information that public criticism inspired the senator's action. The fourth sentence is more likely to be used as a reminder. It presupposes that the reader knows that public criticism inspired someone, perhaps the senator, to vote against the canal project and reminds him (or communicates the new information) that the someone was the senator. In (3) the sentence is arranged so that the reader's attention should focus primarily on the role of public criticism, while in (4) the focus is more on the person voting. Of course, the way that a sentence is interpreted depends also on the sentences around it. These may determine whether sentence (4) is intended to provide a reminder or whether it is assumed to supply new information. In the following passage, the sentence provides a reminder.

> Other legislators have shown themselves unresponsive to the public will. But our senator, although not up for election for five years, defied the party bosses and fought for the eighteen-year-old vote—when the public had indicated its desire to support the measure. When the governor pressured local legislators to ignore the public outcry and support his unnecessary canal project, all but one caved in to the backroom pressure to support it. *It was the senator who was inspired by public criticism to vote against the canal project.*

But in the next passage the same sentence serves a different function, that of imparting new information.

> Only a few of us know what really went on in that committee room. The newspaper claimed that the chairman's vote was the dissenting one that stopped the project. But this is not true. The public outcry had had no effect on him. *It was the senator who was inspired by public criticism to vote against the canal project.*

To a lesser extent, sentences (1) and (2) which follow also differ in focus. The subject position is an important one. In (1) *public criticism* is given more emphasis while in (2) *the senator* is more the focus point. Here again, sentence context is important. The general style and focus of a paragraph influences the style and focus of each sentence within the paragraph. It should be reasonably clear in either of the sentences below:

> Public criticism inspired the senator to vote against the canal project.

> The senator was inspired by public criticism to vote against the canal project.

fits better into this paragraph:

> More recently public criticism has brought about notable changes in the conduct of domestic policy. Public disapproval forced our chief justice to resign. A general discontent with employment policies led to the election of our present junior senator. Public protest made the senator change his mind over indochina.   <u>MISSING SENTENCE</u>   And public censure led him to dismiss his major adviser.

Passive sentences are not necessarily inferior to active ones. If the writer wishes to focus on the logical object of a sentence, the passive form may be better, since in passive sentences the logical object is placed in the important subject position. On the other hand, sentence (1), where the grammatical subject is ''public criticism,'' is a better choice for this paragraph, since the paragraph focus is on the criticism, and every other sentence has the same phrase or a near-paraphrase as its grammatical subject.

EXERCISE

Here are two sentences with the same basic meaning. They sound equally acceptable out of context. What comments can you make about them when placed, one at a time, in the paragraph that follows them?

Sentence 1: He presented to them a large silver medal commemorating the occasion.

Sentence 2: What he presented to them was a large silver medal commemorating the occasion.

Paragraph: Meanwhile a group of loyal Indian leaders in Arizona were invited by the President in 1886 to come to Washington. He received them personally and praised them for their loyalty to the United States.   <u>MISSING SENTENCE</u>

Ambiguity and Dangling Modifiers

Some sentences quite different in form have been shown to share the same basic meaning. Such sentences have been described as basically synonymous. But the reverse situation is not uncommon either—a single sentence may have several basic meanings, as the following ambiguous sentences suggest:

(1)   The police were ordered to stop drinking in the park.

(2)   The lamb was too hot to eat.

(3)   I have always enjoyed entertaining girls.

One reason for the ambiguity of (1) is that the logical object of "stop" and subject of "drinking" could be either "the police" or the indefinite word "anyone." Sentence (2) has two basic meanings:

(1)   *the lamb* is the logical subject of *eat,* the one that does the eating.

(2)   *the lamb* is the logical object of *eat,* the item that someone (anyone) eats.

As for (3), *girls* can be either the logical subject or logical object of *entertaining.* Usually the context makes ambiguous sentences clear, but not always. Unintended ambiguity may distort the writer's meaning:

> Walking along unsteadily we saw the two drunks with pink carnations in their lapels.

A writer must make it quite clear to readers *who* is doing *what* in such a sentence. The sentence above is related to the two quite distinct utterances:

(A)   As we were walking along unsteadily, we saw the two drunks with pink carnations in their lapels.

(B)   As they were walking along unsteadily, we saw the two drunks with pink carnations in their lapels.

A less clumsy version of (*A*) would be:

> We were walking along unsteadily when we saw the two drunks with pink carnations in their lapels.

A less clumsy version of (*B*) would be:

> We saw the two drunks walking along unsteadily with pink carnations in their lapels.

Phrases such as "walking along unsteadily" are known as *reduced forms,* since, although their verbs have no subjects, they are related to longer forms which do have subjects:

> who were walking along unsteadily
> The two drunks were walking along unsteadily.

Such reduced forms are adequate if it is quite clear what their logical subjects are. The second revision

> We saw the two drunks *walking along unsteadily* . . .

is quite clear since the reduced phrase follows its logical subject. But shift the reduced phrase to the beginning:

> *Walking along unsteadily,* we saw the two drunks . . .

and it is not clear whether "we" or "the two drunks" is the logical subject. Reduced phrases which are ambiguous like this are often known as DANGLING MODIFIERS. They dangle because they are not clearly connected to some other element which stands for the omitted subject.

Ambiguity, even distortion, arises quite often when a phrase is misplaced within a sentence. The phrase *to a keeper* is misplaced here

> He handed over a sack worth $40,000 to a keeper.

if the writer did not mean to suggest, say, that only a keeper would value the sack at $40,000 or that only a keeper could get that money for the sack. The phrase *to a keeper* looks as if it gives information about the sack's value when it really identifies the recipient of the sack. A simple way to remedy this is to move *to a keeper* away:

> He handed over to a keeper a sack worth $40,000.

(NOTE: This sentence is only ambiguous when written.)

One other important source of unwanted ambiguity or distortion is the misuse of pronouns like *it, its, this, his:*

> The upheaval in the cities led to unrest in the countryside around. Austrian troops were pelted with stones when they walked alone or in small groups along the country lanes. The peasants were hearing the wildest rumors about events in the cities. *This* resulted in a major change in the direction of policy.

The pronoun could refer to all or only part of the preceding material. Like the modifiers referred to earlier, this pronoun "dangles."

EXERCISE

A. Write an unambiguous revision for each of the following. Where it is useful to show the items responsible for the ambiguity or distortion, the words are italicized.
1. Adam heard God's voice walking in the garden.
2. As soon as Voroshiloff meets the Commissar, we realize that *he* wants only to trap *him.*
3. It is impossible to ignore the influence of music upon man's nature with *its* striving for perfection.
4. Dejected and bleeding all over, the arresting officers found it easy to subdue the Spanish captain.
5. We have examined the spark plugs and fuel lines, which I am sure need cleaning.

B. What interpretations might be drawn from the following:
When Jesus said that he would come to the people, he was really referring to the Holy Spirit.

Subjects and Predicates

Basically an English sentence consists of two parts, one of which serves as the subject, the other as predicate. The subject part contains nouns or nounlike constructions:

> poems
> what Keats wrote
> the article that Trilling criticized
> rumors that the advisers had been evacuated
> candidates in tweed jackets

The predicate part contains a verb, possibly with other words too:

> passed
> denied the accusation
> will report on what they have seen
> used to be corrupt
> were awarding them medals of honor

We'll group nouns like *houses* and *Carol* together with noun-like constructions like *the fact that Sir Andrew hated oysters,* and *the girls in the plaza* and call them NOMINALS (from the Latin *nomen,* "noun"). We'll group together single verbs, verbs with objects, indeed any construction that can act as a predicate and call them VERB PHRASES. Note that a verb phrase may contain one word or several.

So a sentence has a NOMINAL and a VERB PHRASE. This statement can be represented thus:

Here are some sample nominals and verb phrases which can be combined in a number of ways:

```
                        SENTENCE
            _____/_____
           NOMINAL                      VERB PHRASE
              |                              |
           Joseph                         arrived

    the boy with a coat of            was surprising
      many colors

    the youth who had boasted         may have antagonized
      excessively                       Pharaoh

    Joseph's confession               ought to have shaken
                                        everyone

    the news that the family          brought about my surrender
      was in Egypt                      to the authorities
```

Notice that any of the nominals above, which serve as subject,
can also serve as object. In active sentences object nominals are in
the verb phrase and normally follow the verb:

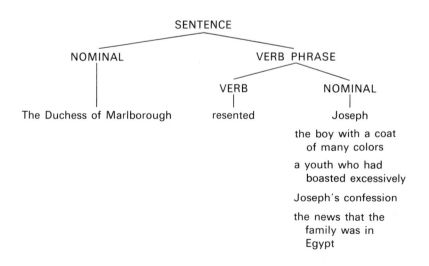

```
                            SENTENCE
              _____/_____
           NOMINAL                        VERB PHRASE
              |                         _____/_____
              |                       VERB          NOMINAL
              |                         |               |
   The Duchess of Marlborough        resented        Joseph

                                                   the boy with a coat
                                                     of many colors

                                                   a youth who had
                                                     boasted excessively

                                                   Joseph's confession

                                                   the news that the
                                                     family was in
                                                     Egypt
```

Indeed, nominals can be objects of prepositions like *about, under, in front of, to, from,* for example:

> The Duchess resented hearing from Miriam
> ABOUT *the news that the family was in Egypt*
>   *Joseph*
>   etc.

and they can serve many other functions not requiring discussion here.

Transformations: Paraphrasing Sentences

A process which changes sentence structure without changing the basic meaning shown in the deep structure is called a TRANS-FORMATION. One such process is the *passive transformation.* This transformation is used to convert the structure of sentences like

> **(1a)** *Joseph* may have antagonized Pharaoh.

> **(2a)** *The news that the family was in Egypt* ought to have shaken everyone.

into sentence structures like those of

> **(1b)** Pharaoh may have been antagonized by *Joseph*.

> **(2b)** Everyone ought to have been shaken by *the news that the family was in Egypt*.

The nominals that were objects in (1*a*) and (2*a*) are subjects in (1*b*) and (2*b*).

NOMINALIZATION

    A special set of transformations converts sentence structures into nominals. Thus the sentence

> Joseph is aggressive.

can be nominalized as

Joseph's being aggressive . . .

or

Joseph's aggressiveness . . .

-ING NOMINALIZATION. In one major type of nominalization, words that are basically verbs take on an -ING ending. These are called *-ING nominals* (or *gerundive nominals*).

Joseph conversed with Sarah.	⟺	Joseph's conversing with Sarah . . .
Kennedy criticized the President	⟺	Kennedy's criticizing (of) the President . . .
Montgomery refused the appointment.	⟺	Montgomery's refusing the appointment. . . .
The prisoners rioted.	⟺	the prisoners' rioting . . .
Jean recognized the truth.	⟺	Jean's recognizing the truth . . .
The doctor removed the glass cover.	⟺	the doctor's removing (of) the glass cover . . .
He loves Glenda.	⟺	his loving Glenda . . .

The subject noun of the sentence becomes a possessive form, and the verb gets an *-ING*. Quite often a preposition like *of* is put before the basic object noun phrase.

An alternative method of -ING nominalization works especially well for some intransitive verbs, i.e., verbs without objects. In this case, *the* appears before the -ING nominal, and the basic subject is preceded by a preposition, *of.*

The mob shouted.	⟺	the shouting of the mob . . .
The bridge collapsed.	⟺	the collapsing of the bridge . . .
Two men drowned.	⟺	the drowning of two men . . .

In the last example the nominal is ambiguous. The reader cannot be sure whether someone drowned the men or whether the men simply drowned. Since -ING nominals may correspond to either active or passive verbs, such ambiguities are not uncommon. The passive meaning can be made explicit with the inclusion of the doer or basic subject in a *by* phrase:

> . . . the drowning of two men by unknown assailants . . .

Transitive verbs (or verbs which take objects) can be nominalized in the same way:

> . . . the looting of the city (by the vandals) . . .

> . . . the manufacturing of amphetamines (by respected drug companies) . . .

-ING nominals sometimes sound clumsy. If they do, they should either be replaced by another kind of nominal, a *derived nominal,* or the writer should change the nominal back to its sentence form. This nominal

> The saturating of the crowd with antipollution literature by this small group . . .

would sound awkward no matter what context it was used in. Better to use the full sentence form:

> This small group saturated the crowd with antipollution literature.

DERIVED NOMINALIZATION. Many verbs and adjectives may be converted into genuine nouns by adding noun endings such as *-action, -al, -ance, -ness,* and *-ism.*

Verb to Noun

SENTENCE		DERIVED NOMINAL
The Romans destroyed the city.	⟺	the destruction of the city (by the Romans) . . .

the Romans' destruction of the city . . .
(cf., the -ING nominal, "the Romans' destroying of the city")

Joseph conversed with Sarah. ⟺ Joseph's conversation with Sarah . . .
(cf., the -ING nominal "Joseph's conversing . . .")

Kennedy criticized the President. ⟺ Kennedy's criticism of the President . . .
(cf., "Kennedy's criticizing . . .")

Montgomery refused the appointment. ⟺ Montgomery's refusal of the appointment.
(cf., "Montgomery's refusing the appointment")

Jean recognized the truth. ⟺ Jean's recognition of the truth . . .
(cf., "Jean's recognizing the truth")

The doctor removed the glass cover. ⟺ the doctor's removal of the glass cover . . .
(cf., "The doctor's removing . . .)

He loves Glenda. ⟺ his love for Glenda . . .
(cf., "his loving Glenda . . .")

They admired Cavour. ⟺ their admiration for Cavour . . .
(cf., "their admiring Cavour . . .")

Adjective to Noun

He was fond of Glenda. ⟺ his fondness for Glenda . . .
(cf., "his being fond of Glenda . . .")

The group was totally unscrupulous.	⟺	the group's total unscrupulousness . . .
They were stupid.	⟺	their stupidity . . .
The advertising was illegal.	⟺	the illegality of the advertising . . .
The Senate was reluctant.	⟺	the Senate's reluctance . . .

SENTENCE AND NOMINALS. For our purposes it is convenient to relate nominals to sentences by transformations. But this does not mean that the speaker or writer really goes through such processes when using the language or that a more theoretically oriented grammar would describe them in the same way. Derived nominals do not necessarily have the same meaning as the corresponding -ING nominal. Thus, "criticizing a book" is not necessarily equivalent to a "criticism of a book" (which may be a published article). In this case, as in many others, the derived nominal *criticism* is the RESULT of the activity represented by the -ING nominal *criticizing.*

Nevertheless, when a writer is revising a first draft, an awareness of the existence of these alternatives may be very useful, together with some insight into meaning differences resulting from the surface form of a sentence.

In the following student passage the use of short sentences with unnominalized verbs makes the events seem immediate, ongoing, alive.

> The waves crashed. The wind howled. The lifeboat rocked perilously. All this drove us into a state of frenzied terror.

Converting the verbs into -ING nominals deprives the events of their immediacy, their "ungoingness."

> The crashing of the waves, the howling of the wind, and the perilous rocking of the lifeboat all drove us into a state of frenzied terror.

However, the cause-effect link receives extra focus. The events are ''distanced'' by the nominalizations and appear more as links in a chain—this, this, and this event caused that state. In fact, there are degrees of ''ungoingness.'' So in

> Huck admired Jim. This changed his attitude towards the man he had once regarded as a chattel.

the *admiring* gets more focus because it is a full verb in a separate sentence. Nominalize it and embed it in the second sentence, and the focus is reduced:

> Huck's admiring Jim changed his attitude towards the man he had once regarded as a chattel.

And here again the cause-effect idea link is strengthened. But the energy of the *admiring* can be further reduced by using a derived nominal instead of the -ING form. By this means an event is reduced to a fact:

> Huck's admiration for Jim changed his attitude towards the man he had once regarded as a chattel.

Here the writer takes for granted Huck's feeling for Jim and strengthens further the focus on the cause-effect idea link.

One kind of grammatical construction is not superior in itself to another. The writer's purposes have to influence the sentence choices he makes.

One problem with nominalization is that it can all too easily be misused. The result, sometimes a deliberate result, is often the kind of clumsy academic or bureaucratic jargon that confuses the reader:

> (1a) The gain of local control for communities is only achievable through the transference of political power from the mayor to the councilmen.

> (2a) Marx's conception of the inevitability of middle-class domination over the workers is comprehensible only on the

basis of our acceptance of the correctness of his belief in the purely economic causality of political change.

Such prose can be clarified by converting the nominalized elements like *gain, transference, conception, domination, acceptance,* and *causality* into verbs:

> **(1b)** Communities can gain local control only if political power is transferred from the mayor to the councilmen.

> **(2b)** Marx thought that the middle class would inevitably dominate the workers. We can understand this only if we accept his belief that economics alone causes political change.

Now it is considerably easier to find out who does what and under what conditions. Both unskilled writer and deceitful persuaders may overuse these very useful nominalizing processes.

EXERCISE

The following sentences contain some nominalized forms where unnominalized forms might be better. Rephrase the sentences to improve them.

1. My belief is that a person's active involvement in civic affairs can often result in the learning of valuable skills.
2. A decision was made by the participants to force a Spanish withdrawal from the Netherlands.
3. The choice of a site for the installation of a radar scanner was finally arrived at by the Council of Ministers.
4. The play's rejection by the critics was the effect of uninspired direction.
5. Mary showed a deterioration in health during the next year.
6. An excessive concentration on vocational training by the administration was noticed by the commissioners' report.

EMBEDDING

The nominalizations discussed above were described as originating from independent sentences. Once nominalized, they may serve, like other nominals, as subject, object, and so forth. They can be shown at different levels of language:

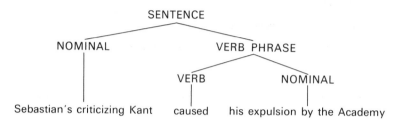

The diagram above represents the surface structure or form of the sentence. At an earlier, more basic, stage the sentence might be shown this way:

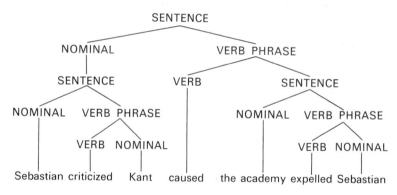

Grammarians often use this more basic stage as a way of showing meaning relations. Compare this tree with the actual sentence:

> Sebastian's criticizing Kant caused his expulsion by the Academy.

At the deeper level, at which the more basic meaning relations are shown, the main sentence is shown to contain embedded within it two other sentences or propositions:

> Sebastian criticized Kant.

> The Academy expelled Sebastian.

Sentence embedding is common in English, as in every other known language and there are many ways of doing it. Suppose the sentence

> Galahad had arrived late.

is to be embedded as the subject of another sentence:

> <u>(something)</u>   surprised Lancelot.

One possibility is to convert the Galahad sentence into a derived nominal:

> Galahad's late arrival surprised Lancelot.

Alternatively the -ING construction might be used:

> Galahad's having arrived late surprised Lancelot.

Note here the possessive ending on the subject and the *-ing* ending on the first part of the verb phrase.

But instead of embedding with *'s . . . -ing,* a writer could choose *infinitive embedding,* using *for* in front of the subject and *to* in front of the verb:

> *For* Galahad *to* have arrived late surprised Lancelot.

Or a writer might choose clause embedding, using the embedding word *that:*

> *That* Galahad had arrived late surprised Lancelot.

Use the invented term *embedder* for elements like *'s . . . -ing, for . . . to,* and *that,* which are used to embed one sentence structure inside another:

Gerundive Embedder: possessive . . . *-ing*

Infinitive Embedder: *for . . . to*

Clause Embedder: *that*

The Galahad sentences above differ little if at all in meaning. But this isn't always true:

(A)   She hated (*for*) Carl *to* cheat that man.

(B)   She hated Carl's cheat*ing* that man.

The (*B*) sentence implies that Carl may really have cheated the man, whereas the (*A*) sentence allows more easily the possibility that Carl did not actually cheat him.

Not all verbs can be followed by all kinds of embedders. The verb *know* allows only the clause and infinitive embedding:

> I know you *to* be an honest man. (The *for* part of *for . . . to* often has to be deleted.)

> I know *that* you are an honest man.

Ungrammatical: I know your being an honest man.

EXTRAPOSITION

The sentence

> That Galahad had arrived early surprised Lancelot.

is a little clumsy. The embedded sentence together with its embedder *that* may be moved out of its position to a place at the end of the sentence:

> ___surprised Lancelot *that Galahad had arrived early.*

Since *surprised* has no subject, a pronoun empty of meaning—*it*—has to be introduced. This *it* stands for the embedded sentence.

> *It* surprised Lancelot *that Galahad had arrived early.*

The process of shifting an embedded sentence in this way is called *extraposition.* Extraposition is used for other kinds of embedded sentences:

INFINITIVE NOMINAL

> *For him to do that* was unusual.   It was unusual *for him to do that.*

RELATIVE CLAUSE

A boy *who wanted to join the Peace corps* came.

A boy came *who wanted to join the Peace Corps.*

Extraposition often makes a sentence more readable and easier to understand:

Not extraposed: *That Peer Gynt should have stood up to the Button-mender instead of evading him* now seems clear.

Extraposed: It now seems clear *that Peer Gynt should have stood up to the Button-mender instead of evading him.*

EXERCISE

Try extraposing the following sentences. In which of these sentences does extraposing make for much greater clarity?

About the other sentences—those for which the different versions are almost equally clear—make some comments about any difference you notice in the focus of each version.

1. That the medieval community of scholars developed into the modern vocational schools for lawyers and schoolteachers seems strange. (Begin *It seems . . .*)
2. For the government to impose controls was unthinkable for those who had always believed that unbridled private enterprise would always be an essential part of American life. (Begin *It was . . . .* Then begin another version with *For those who . . .*)
3. That she was indeed guilty was not doubted by any state or federal law enforcement office although proofs were still lacking. (Begin *It was not . . . .* Then try to write a third version superior to both of these versions.)

Pronouns, Meaning, and Reference

An embedded sentence serves as the object nominal in the following structure, which underlies two possible sentences, only one of which refers to Garibaldi.

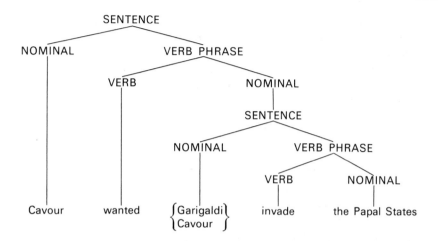

If the infinitive embedder *for . . . to* is used, the following sentence structures are produced:

(1a) Cavour wanted for Garibaldi to invade the Papal States.

(2a) Cavour wanted for Cavour to invade the Papal States.

The *for* part of the infinitive embedder is almost always removed in such sentences except for a few spoken dialects:

(1b) Cavour wanted Garibaldi to invade the Papal States.

(2b) Cavour wanted Cavour to invade the Papal States.

Although (1*b*) and (2*b*) have the same grammatical structure, only (1*b*) is a grammatical sentence of English. To make (2*b*) grammatical, the second reference to Cavour must be omitted:

(2c) Cavour wanted to invade the Papal States.

In (1*b*) *Garibaldi* is the logical subject of *invade,* but it cannot be deleted without altering the meaning. However, the logical subject of *invade* in (2*b*) is *Cavour,* and this can be deleted without altering the meaning. The relevant differences between (1*b*) and (2*b*) is that in (2*b*) the logical subjects of *wanted* and *invade* are the same. So there is a transformation which deletes a nominal if it is identical in reference to an earlier one. This condition of identity is an important one in language. If and only if the logical subject and object of a verb are identical, a reflexive pronoun (*myself, himself,* etc.) replaces the basic object:

(3a) Empson contradicted Empson.

(3b) Empson contradicted him.

(3c) Empson contradicted himself.

Sentence (3*a*) cannot be understood as if the subject and object nominals refer to the same person, nor can (3*b*). Only the use of the reflexive in (3*c*) indicates this kind of identity.

However, when the identity of reference holds for nominals which are *not* subjects or objects of the same verb, then a reflexive pronoun is not used. Instead, personal or possessive pronouns (*he, him, his, she, her, they, it, them, their*) are used.

So,

(4a) *Empson* claimed that *Empson* had been wrong.

(4b) *Empson* claimed that *Empson's* book had been wrong.

(4c) *Empson* claimed that Leavis had misunderstood *Empson.*

have to be transformed into:

(5a) Empson claimed that *he* had been wrong.

(5b) Empson claimed that *his* book had been wrong.

(5c) Empson claimed that Leavis had misunderstood *him.*

For readers and writers, as we saw earlier, sentences like (5*a, b,* and *c*) are sometimes a problem because the pronouns are ambiguous. The pronouns *he, his,* and *him* do not have to represent *Empson.* They might refer to some other person mentioned in a previous sentence. Writers, especially writers of tightly organized logical arguments, have to take especial care to eliminate such ambiguities before the final draft of an article or paper. Note the difficulty in interpreting *this* in the following passage:

> Mazzini pointed out that Cavour's cautiousness had led to widespread dissatisfaction with the slowness of the campaign momentum. *This* was to be a significant factor in the unification of Italy.

The pronoun *this* might refer to the widespread dissatisfaction or to the slowness of momentum or to Mazzini's pointing all this out, or to Cavour's cautiousness or, maybe, just to the campaign momentum without any reference to slowness.

MORE ON DELETION

Deletion processes do not just apply to nominals identical in reference to some other nominal. Indefinite words like *someone* or *anyone* can often be deleted without changing basic meaning relationships:

(1a) This solution is hard for anyone to evaluate.

(1b) This solution is hard to evaluate.

(2a) He knew that the circuits had been destroyed by someone.

(2b) He knew that the circuits had been destroyed.

The (*a*) sentences are not, of course, completely synonymous with the (*b*) sentences. The indefinite nominals *anyone* and *someone* are somehow more definite in reference than is the absence of any word at all. But notice that passive sentences, for example, can be written with an indefinite "someone" as their logical subject:

> This matter can be arranged *by someone.*

or without any words representing the logical subject:

> This matter can be arranged.

The second of these can be used by those who hope to avoid questions as to *who* would do the arranging. A politician mentioning the *someone* might be more likely to be asked who the *someone* is than one who omits the *by someone* phrase.

Nor is deletion restricted to nominals. Another kind of deletion removes verbs or adjectives identical in reference to some others. Sometimes this deletion is optional:

> (3a) Samuelson *provided* the initial evidence, and Schlesinger *provided* the later material.
>
> (3b) Samuelson provided the initial evidence and Schlesinger the later material.
>
> (4a) Fletcher was *shrewd,* and his brother was *shrewd* too.
>
> (4b) Fletcher was shrewd, and his brother was too.
>
> (4c) Fletcher was shrewd, and so was his brother.

Sometimes, as in comparatives, the deletion is obligatory and covers more than single elements:

> (5a) Dulles' *evaluation of the European situation was* more *pessimistic* than my *evaluation of the European situation was pessimistic.*

Here are four possible surface structures of the Dulles example. In each case some elements identical in reference to others have been deleted.

> (5b) Dulles' evaluation of the European situation was more pessimistic than my evaluation of the European situation.
>
> (5c) Dulles' evaluation of the European situation was more pessimistic than my evaluation.
>
> (5d) Dulles' evaluation of the European situation was more pessimistic than mine was.
>
> (5e) Dulles' evaluation of the European situation was more pessimistic than mine.

Note that when the possessive pronouns *my, your, her, our,* and *their* are not immediately followed by nouns, they become *mine, yours, hers, ours,* and *theirs* respectively. Similarly, if deletions leave only a single personal pronoun after *than,* like *I, he, she, we,* and *they,* these are often changed to *me, him, her, us,* and *them* respectively. Thus

> He is brighter than she is (bright).

can be reduced to either the infrequent

> He is brighter than she.

or the more common

> He is brighter than her.

There is a danger of ambiguity in this kind of reduction since

> **(6)**   They like Bach better than the critics like Bach.

and

> **(7)**   They like Bach better than they like the critics.

can both be reduced by deletion to

> **(8)**   They like Bach better than the critics.

It is not clear in (8) whether *the critics* is really the logical subject or the logical object of *like.*

EXERCISE

Read the following items and decide if certain pronouns or deletions have made the message unclear. Revise where necessary.

1. During the meeting with Montgomery, Eisenhower argued that he should lead the invasion forces into Italy.
2. Wildcats eat rabbits more often than coyotes.
3. Claiming that Macbeth had really killed his father-in-law, not the king, the critic argued that his sons must have killed the king.

4. Humming quietly as if in deep thought, Alice saw a white rabbit.

Monster Sentences

We have been demonstrating alternative ways of expressing the same basic meanings. The choice is the writer's and he will be judged, in part, by his choices. Obviously an unnecessarily complicated sentence is worse than several separate simple ones. At one extreme is the overuse of short, jerky sentences not clearly related to each other. At the other extreme are monster sentences like this:

> That Bertolucci is aware of the fact that the equation of politics with sex is extremely complex is apparent in his having changed the Moravia ending in such a way that the entire film is ultimately modified by ambiguity. It is also apparent in Bertolucci's cinematic style, which is so rich, poetic and baroque that it is simply incapable of meaning only what it says—and which is, I think, a decided improvement over Moravia's sometimes tiresomely lean prose.
>
> —Vincent Canby, "Film: 'The Conformist'"

EXERCISE

Make the following sentences more readable and clear:

1. By believing a just and moral cause, such as the eradication of war, justifies the denial of opportunities to participate in war research and ROTC on college campuses, the protestors against war research fall into just the trap Nietzsche warned of, for they take on the old practice of denying basic freedoms when those freedoms come in conflict with the aims of society.
2. Even if the government refused to use its mechanical systems solely for the national defense, the government is maintaining an army which is disproportionate to its need to defend itself, since we are not under attack or at war, or its responsibility to other nations as agreed upon as a result of the myriad of post-World War II defense treaties.

Sentences, Clauses, and Fragments

Near the beginning of this section we showed that English sentences normally had to have a nominal (serving as subject) and a verb phrase (serving as predicate). In fact, there is another important requirement in determining whether a string of words is or is not a sentence. The verb phrase must be a *finite verb phrase.*

A finite verb phrase contains either an auxiliary verb (*will, may, was, have, could, did,* etc.) before the verb, or the simple verb in the present or past tense. The following contain finite verb phrases. The verbs in them are italicized:

(1) The English *had acquired* a good reputation abroad as metalworkers.

(2) Because they *had* this reputation, their work *was* popular.

Here are some verb phrases which are *not* finite. The verbs are again italicized. Note that without a finite verb phrase these strings of words are not grammatical sentences:

(3) the English *having acquired* a good reputation as metalworkers . . .

(4) their work *being* popular on account of this reputation . . .

Each part of a sentence containing a subject nominal and a finite verb phrase is called a *clause.* Here are two kinds of clauses:

A	B
(5) The monopoly raises the rate of mercantile profit.	because the monopoly raises the rate of mercantile profit.
	after the monopoly raises the rate of mercantile profit.
	although the monopoly raises the rate of mercantile profit.
(6) But it diminishes the sum total of the revenue.	which diminishes the sum total of the revenue.

> while it diminishes the sum
> total of the revenue.
>
> so that it diminishes the sum
> total of the revenue.

The clauses on the left can serve as grammatical sentences of English. The clauses on the right cannot. They all have embedders such as *because, although, so that,* which might be called clause embedders, and require the addition of another clause without embedders if they are to become full sentences. Such embedded clauses are often called *subordinate clauses* because they are below the level of full sentences. The others are called *independent, principal,* or *main clauses.*

Conjoining, Subordinating, and Focusing

Instead of embedding one clause in another, the writer can use conjunctions like *and* or *but* to join them together. This process is called *conjoining.* By this means, two clauses can receive approximately equal emphasis:

(1a)   Monopoly raises profit rates, $\begin{Bmatrix} \text{and} \\ \text{but} \end{Bmatrix}$ competition reduces prices.

(2a)   He came across a poet who had rejected the traditional forms and who had developed a new kind of epic.

Notice that there are two mentions of *who had* in (2a). The second mention can be deleted since it is identical with the first:

(2b)   He came across a poet who had rejected the traditional forms and developed a new kind of epic.

Notice that deletion would have been possible in (1a) if the two clauses had contained identical subject nominals. So

(3a)   Monopoly raises profit rates, but monopoly reduces efficiency.

can be transformed into

> **(3b)**   Monopoly raises profit rates but reduces efficiency.

SUBORDINATION AND FOCUS

In general, in sentences with both main and subordinate clauses, the sentence focus is on the main clause. Indeed, any kind of embedding leads to some de-emphasizing of the content of the embedded constructions. Contrast the following sentences:

> **(1a)**   De Gaulle took offense because he had not been notified in advance.

> **(1b)**   The reason for de Gaulle's taking offense was that he had not been notified in advance.

Both sentences share the same basic meaning. But the reason for de Gaulle's feeling is given less emphasis in (1*a*) because it is in a subordinate clause.

There are two useful ways to vary further the emphasis of (1*b*):

> **(1c)**   *What* caused de Gaulle to take offense *was* the lack of advance notification.

> **(1d)**   *It was* the lack of advance notification *that* caused de Gaulle to take offense.

Both (1*c*) and (1*d*) represent a kind of sentence known as a *cleft* sentence. Both sentences are really split up (cleft) versions of the sentence:

> **(1e)**   The lack of advance notification caused de Gaulle to take offense.

The subject part of (1*e*), *the lack of advance notification,* has been separated or cleft from the predicate part, *caused de Gaulle to take offense,* by the word *was* in (*c*) and *that* in (*d*). The cleft sentence beginning with *what* allows the focus to be on the material after *was.* The one beginning with *it was* places the focus of the sentence on the material immediately following *was,* i.e., the original subject nominal, not the verb phrase. Note the following cleft sentences in which the focus is on a human being:

(1f)   The $\begin{Bmatrix} \text{one} \\ \text{person} \\ \text{leader} \\ \text{etc.} \end{Bmatrix}$ who was most offended at this lack

of advance notification was de Gaulle.

In all of these cases the cleft constructions are used to "sharpen" the writing by providing appropriate emphasis. But again a warning is appropriate: overuse reduces the impact, and careless use results in uneconomical writing.

RELATIVE CLAUSES AND DELETION

The sentence (1f) can be replaced by a sentence without the words *who was,* for example,

(1g)   The one most offended at this lack of advance notification was de Gaulle.

In fact, any relative clause beginning with a relative pronoun subject like *who, which, that* followed by a form of *be* (*is, are, was, were*) can be reduced to a phrase by deleting the relative pronoun and the *be* form. So,

(2a)   The doctor who was waiting in the garden . . .

becomes

(2b)   The doctor waiting in the garden . . .

Similarly the relative clause in

(3a)   This situation, which was more serious than Louis had expected, frightened the French leaders.

can be reduced to the phrase in

(3b)   This situation, more serious than Louis had expected, frightened the French leaders.

A clause, remember, contains a subject nominal and a finite verb phrase. The subject nominal in relative clauses may be the relative pronoun itself (*who, which, that*), or a possessive relative pronoun with a noun:

> (4a)   Marlborough, *whose armies* were already menacing Paris . . .

These are reduced differently. The possessive relative pronoun *whose* loses its ''relativeness'' and becomes the ordinary possessive, *his*. The form of *be* (*were*) is deleted in the usual way:

> (4b)   Marlborough, his armies already menacing Paris . . .

In addition to Relative Clause Reduction, another transformation is needed when the relative clause has only an adjective after *be.* This so-called Adjective Transformation shifts an adjective to the position in front of the noun in the main clause. Thus, by Relative Clause Reduction, we transform:

> (5a)   I saw a general who was furious storming towards me.

into the ungrammatical

> (5b)   I saw a general furious storming towards me.

which has to become, by the Adjective Transformation:

> (5c)   I saw a furious general storming towards me.

Useful as Relative Clause Reduction is in making prose more compact, it often has another effect. The content of the clause is pushed a little further into the background when the clause is reduced. Look back at (2a), (3a), (4a), and (5a) and compare them with (2b), (3b), (4b), and (5c).

REDUCTION OF TIME CLAUSES

Much the same kind of reduction process may be used to transform

> (1a)   As I was looking over the document, I could not help exclaiming in surprise.

into

> (1b)   Looking over the document, I could not help exclaiming in surprise.

But in this case not only is the time embedder *as* deleted, along with *was,* but also the subject nominal *I,* which is identical in reference to the subject of the main clause *I could not help . . .*

Ambiguities or distortions arise if a subject nominal is deleted which does not have the same reference as a nominal in the main clause. Thus, the following sentence is quite clear:

> (2a)   As I was looking at the trees, Joseph walked away with my suitcase.

but the clause reduction transformation results in a distortion of the author's meaning:

> (2b)   Looking at the trees, Joseph walked away with my suitcase.

The following is unambiguous:

> (3a)   As I was looking at the trees, Joseph hit me with a half-empty milk bottle.

but it becomes distorted, possibly ambiguous, in this form:

> (3b)   Looking at the trees, Joseph hit me with a half-empty milk bottle.

Sometimes the result of careless clause reduction is ridiculous. The sentence

> (4a)   As I was looking at the trees, a flash of lightning struck the largest.

becomes

> (4b)   Looking at the trees, a flash of lightning struck the largest.

Phrases like *looking at the trees* in (2*b*), (3*b*), and (4*b*) and *looking over the document* in (1*b*) are often called *participial phrases.* But in (2*b*), (3*b*), and (4*b*) they are *dangling phrases.* They lack a nominal in the main clause that clearly stands for the logical subject of the participle. The phrase is "dangling" without a logical subject.

More About Focus

It seems that embedding a sentence as a clause reduces the emphasis assigned to its content. Reducing it from a clause with a finite verb phrase to a phrase without one pushes it yet further into the background. A similar reduction of emphasis is achieved by nominalization. Conversely, emphasis on particular parts of a sentence can be heightened by transforming them into the appropriate cleft sentence. We have called this heightening of emphasis *focus.*

The transformations described in this grammar section are not intended to serve as tools for the first draft of a paper. If used as such, they may either inhibit creative thinking and exploration or they will confuse the writer and his writing. They are intended as revision techniques. After the writer has checked his organization and worked out a carefully directed second draft, he can then profitably use the processes described here to check his sentences and to clarify or strengthen them wherever he finds this desirable. The grammar presents an array of choices for the writer who knows where he is going.

Word Choice

Student writers often find it very difficult to choose words that are right for what they have to say. This section is intended to help you choose words which clarify your message rather than distort it. Traditional rules of usage are given here in simplified form. This section is also intended to show how complex many other rules of usage are, rules that rarely appear in any dictionary or grammar text.

One of the difficulties is that many writers think they must follow rules such as these:

1. Descriptive or vivid words like *gallop, trudge,* or *charge* are better than plain words like *go*. [This is oversimplified partly because it is difficult to say just what descriptive words are. Adjectives of taste or color or sound can make dull writing come alive, but used without reason they can, of course, detract from the writer's intended meaning.]

2. Long words and abstract words like *elucidate* or *inasmuch* give a paper a certain dignity so that the paper may be taken seriously. They also create a necessary distance between the writer and his message. [This is not always true. Simple clear words may also lend dignity to a piece of writing. Language should be clear, direct, and as simple as the message will allow. A writer rarely needs to create distance between himself and what he says. Except for specialized kinds of scientific or legal writing, simple, noncolloquial words are preferable.]

When choosing words try not to rely on such laws and formulas, but concentrate instead on the context of your writing. Be aware that one word is never the same as another in every respect.

Words and Implication

If you describe a man as *accusing* another of some action, you are taking it for granted that the accuser believes the action to be bad. Thus if you change the following sentence

> Lawyers *said* that Smith controlled the airline.

to

> Lawyers *accused* Smith of controlling the airline.

you have implied something quite different in the second sentence from what you have implied in the first. Compare the two versions below:

> (A) Lawyers *claimed* that Smith controlled the airline.
> (B) Lawyers *realized* that Smith controlled the airline.

It is clear that in the two sentences the lawyers are "doing" something different. In (*A*) they *claimed.* In (*B*) they *realized.* But now turn your attention to the writer of these sentences, some unknown person. From what he has written, does it appear that he assumes that Smith controlled the airline, or is he unsure about this? Read the sentences again. In (*A*) the writer does *not* reveal

any belief of his own that Smith really did control the airline. But
(*B*) does communicate such a belief. In (*B*) it is not just the lawyers who believe that Smith controlled the airline—the writer of
the sentence believes it too.

The point may be clearer if you think of the verb "know"
(similar to "realize") and what it implies about the person who
uses the word in speech or writing. Can you say

> Irma knew that Columbus sailed to America in 1967.

—not unless you put quotation marks around "knew," or not unless there is some modern figure named Columbus. If you use
"know" in the ordinary sense, you—the speaker or writer—are
assuming that what is *known,* by Harry, or Irma, or any other subject, is true. If you did not assume this, you would not use the
verb "know," but some other verb like "thought" or "supposed."
The interesting point about all of this is the light it can shed on a
writer. If someone writes:

> Sister Carrie found out that the big city uses human beings and in
> the end destroys them.

he, the writer, implies by the use of "found out" that he also believes in the destructiveness of the big city. By changing the verb
to "came to believe" he would not imply that he necessarily
shared the belief.

EXERCISE

Point out the differences, if any, between the (*a*) and (*b*) sentences
below:

1a. Kennan understands that we must deal promptly with aggression.
1b. Kennan believes that we must deal promptly with aggression.
2a. She perceived that Roger had already reported the accident.
2b. She believed that Roger had already reported the accident.
3a. An analysis of Plato's theories of education shows that they

have played a major role in the development of modern educational theory.

3b. An analysis of Plato's theories of education suggests that they
have played a major role in the development of modern educational theory.

4a. He had noticed that the memorandum had been forged.

4b. He had asserted that the memorandum had been forged.

Jargon

Words and phrases like *intrasystemic feedback, inferiority complex,
median income, logical inference, imperialism, recession, depression, reinforcement of behavior* have fairly precise meanings within
the technical disciplines to which they belong. But they can be
unclear and misleading in more general use.

A jargon is a vocabulary of words and phrases used by spe-
cialists to make technical discussion in their specialization more
compact and precise. Unfortunately, such a jargon may also be
used as a way to shut off outsiders from a discipline or to impress.
The following is a legitimate use of jargon:

> If morphemes are defined in terms of phonemes, and, simultaneously, morpho-
> logical considerations are considered relevant to phonemic analysis, then linguis-
> tic theory may be nullified by a real circularity.
>
> —Noam Chomsky, *Syntactic Structures*

In the context in which it appeared—a technical linguistic discussion of how to formulate grammars—this is compact, precise, and
understandable to linguists.

But the same cannot be said for the following public report on
foreign language training by the government. The writer was try-
ing to report that some supervisors thought instructors' comments
should be included with both major examination results and minor
quizzes. Apparently not everyone had agreed:

> It was observed that there was a dichotomy of opinion with regard to
> tabulation of macro-success levels discernible at higher administrational
> levels concerned with implementation of the aforementioned evaluation

procedures. It was felt by some that although anecdotative as well as quantitative data had been purposefully incorporated into micro-success level reporting, such data were also desirable if the less micro-task oriented evaluations were to have meaningful dimensions.

The language here is an inflated jargon designed to impress rather than to communicate real information about language testing procedures.

Such an abuse of jargon is often labeled "gobbledygook" or occasionally "officialese," but public officials are not the only ones who use it. You will easily recognize it from its official, impersonal, even dehumanized tone, its complicated sentences, and its overuse of long words.

Euphemisms

A euphemism is an expression used as a substitute for words that might be distasteful or embarrassing. In 1793 a decapitation was called a "shorn crown." Today a prison is a "correctional institution." A bombing attack can be a "protective reaction strike" and stealing by employees has been called "inventory leakage."

Such words are an attempt, conscious or unconscious, to protect both writers and readers from some part of the reality. If a friend "passes on," the implication is that he has not really *died* but has merely gone to another existence. *Sleeping pills* suggest drugs—possible addiction, possible overdose, possible death—but "nighttime medication" is almost free of such unpleasant suggestions. And "ripping off" implies that there is no victim, as there would be if somebody had been *robbing* or *burglarizing.* The phrase suggests that the original owner (frequently an institution) had no real need for the item which was "ripped off."

Occasionally a euphemism is so ingrained in the language that it is impossible to avoid. You should try, however, to become aware of euphemisms, and, where possible, to seek more exact, more direct words which will better fit the context of your writing.

Pompous Words

Certain old pompous phrases like "the rewards of virtue," "the path of knowledge," "on the highway of life" are not likely to be produced nowadays. But there is a modern equivalent which almost everyone produces at some time or another. The sentences below were written by a freshman student who was describing his efforts to compose some experimental music. The translations are the student's explanations.

> The instruments I employed in my piece were difficult to choose because I truly had no conception of my musical production.

Translation: It was difficult to choose the instruments because I had no idea how I wanted my musical production to sound.

> The project was nebulous and my understanding was even more unformulated.

Translation: I did not understand what I was supposed to do.

> My *modus operandi* was quite unusual and unique.

Translation: My approach was unique.

> I desired that an enhancing characteristic of my piece would be style and continuity.

Translation: I wanted my piece to have style and continuity.

The existence of the translations should make it easier for the student to evaluate the content of his writing. He may decide to change several of the sentences still further.

In a desire to sound professional, many writers lose control of their language. Not only do the big fancy words sound pompous but many of them are used wrongly as well. The following ungrammatical sentences were written by sane and sensible native speakers of the language who simply lost hold of what they wanted to say:

I for one believe the Bible should be read with an objective point of view and believe certain things to be questionable as factual.

Student Revision: Parts of the Bible are not literally true.

It is a well known fact that early man signified natural phenomena with something invisible or intangible to his knowledge.

Student Revision: Early man invented invisible spirits or gods to explain the occurrence of mysterious natural phenomena like lightning.

The fact that I was learning to speak Spanish created quite an impressive experience for me.

Student Revision: I was pleased to be learning how to speak Spanish.

It is drama that shows how some situations are incapable of being avoided by tragedy.

Student Revision: Drama shows that in some situations tragedy is unavoidable.

Man is a product of his own destruction.

Student Revision: Some men have destroyed themselves.

Ordinarily the cure for such word use is simply to read the whole paper aloud, spot the strange-sounding sentence, and rephrase it. If, however, a sentence like one of those above does not sound strange to him, the writer is probably not familiar enough with the words to know how they can and cannot be used in particular contexts. The next section explains how grammatical context limits one's choice of words.

Words and Grammatical Context

Each word learned by a speaker of a language carries with it many little rules, and while such rules are hardly ever written down, they are nevertheless in effect. For example, people say

> She composed a symphony.

but some semantic rule prevents them from saying

> She composed a novel.

even though ''compose'' can mean *to write* and one can *write a novel.* The existence of such rules explains why synonyms in a dictionary or in a thesaurus are not always interchangeable. *Develop* and *evolve* are sometimes synonyms but only *develop* can go in the blank here:

> Hemingway was able to _____ a clean, uncluttered style.

As for *evolve:* man *evolved,* a theory can *evolve,* and the British Constitution *evolved* from centuries of court precedents. *Develop* can be used wherever *evolve* is used—man *evolved* or man *developed*—but *evolve* cannot be used everywhere that *develop* is used. The verb *evolve* does not allow an object—''Hemingway evolved a style'' is wrong—but *develop* can be used with or without an object. (A theory can *develop,* or scientists can *develop a theory.*)

Consider also the synonyms *aggravated* and *worsened.* Only *worsened* will fit in the blank below:

> Mrs. Hale's condition _____ daily.

whereas *aggravated* might be used in the following context:

> The damp air _____ Mrs. Hale's condition.

The verb *worsen* cannot take an object. It is ungrammatical to say ''The doctor worsened my illness.'' *Aggravate,* on the other hand, cannot be used *without* an object. ''My lumbago aggravated everyday'' is wrong. So is ''The tension in the office aggravated.''

Such examples show that some verbs do not allow objects; other verbs require an object; and still others allow an object but do not require it.

A larger dictionary sometimes supplies this kind of information about context by means of example sentences, but dictionary space is limited. The larger the dictionary, the more sentences can be provided, and so the closer it can come to giving a complete picture of the contexts in which the word is used.

There are occasions when a word is wrong, and an educated native speaker senses that it is wrong. But he may have difficulty seeing why the word is wrong. Here are a few examples illustrating rules that, if violated, make a sentence "sound wrong."

Example 1:	The boycott method was proven in a strike organized by Chavez and the Farm Workers Union.
Correction:	The boycott method $\begin{Bmatrix} \text{was proven} \\ \text{was proved} \end{Bmatrix}$ effective in a strike organized by Chavez and the Farm Workers Union.
Probable Rule:	This usage of *prove* requires a statement of what is proved. You cannot *prove* a thing, only a statement about a thing.

Example 2:	a.	The purpose of the Inquisition was to investigate heresy, contended to be brought about by contacts with non-Christians.
	b.	Kissinger did not contend the glorification of war.
Correction:	a.	The purpose of the Inquisition was to investigate heresy, which, the Inquisition contended, had been brought about by contacts with non-Christians.
	b.	Kissinger did not contend that war was glorious.
Probable Rule:		The verb *contend* is often used to mean "advance an opinion in an argument." It must normally be followed by *that,* not a noun [or nominalization, as

in (*b*)], and not an infinitive with *to,* as in (*a*). In complicated sentences like (*a*) it is easy for a writer to lose his language feel. You can use *argue* instead. The strangeness of this sentence might have been more evident had it been read aloud.

Example 3:	The nature of the soul in Plato's *Republic* is a secondary but vital aspect in his discussion of justice.
Correction:	The nature of the soul in Plato's *Republic* is a secondary but vital theme in his discussion of justice.
Probable Rule:	The word *aspect* normally takes the preposition *of: an aspect of Plato's thought.* However, this word is frequently used wrongly as a general term meaning *topic, theme,* or *concern.*

Many of these abstract words are easily misused by student writers. The usage rules are complicated and different for each word. Thus *insight* can be *given* only to a human being. But it has to be *contributed* to a problem. You cannot hope to learn all such rules. Familiarity with them comes from much reading. In the meantime, if you are unsure about them, use more specific terms and rephrase your sentences. A more specific statement may well be superior to one with *aspect* or *insight* used correctly.

EXERCISE

Each of the following sentences should "sound wrong" to a native speaker of English. Rewrite the sentence and write a probable rule for each, in the manner of the boxed-in examples. If any of these do not sound wrong, then your own internal grammar of English is, to some slight degree, incomplete. Consult a big dictionary or a verbal friend. Try to find out which words "sound wrong."

1. That suit becomes her constantly
2. Hotspur's intervention deteriorated the situation considerably.
3. The atmosphere ameliorated slightly when the presents were brought in.
4. The poet relates a part of human nature familiar to everyone.

Prepositions

When you revise a paper, look for prepositions like *in, on, with, from,* and *to* which sound strange when the work is read aloud. The sentence

> The writer deals on the idea of free choice.

should be changed to

> The writer deals *with* the idea of free choice.

The phrase

> interested with people

should be

> interested *in* people

With phrases as familiar as these, your own language intuition should enable you to spot the mistakes and correct them. In cases where you are not sure, or if you find a preposition circled on your paper, then look up the whole phrase in a dictionary. *Analogy,* for example, can take *with:*

> He was the first to make the *analogy* of earth *with* a spaceship.

but *analogous* takes *to:*

> Earth is *analogous to* a spaceship in several respects.

(At this point the writer should consider whether *analogous to* is better than *like* in the context of the piece of writing.)

Prepositions in some cases can change the whole character of a sentence. Think of the verb *treat,* for example, and the ways in which different prepositions will change its meaning:

treat *with:* The doctor *treated* the sickness *with* aspirin and penicillin.

The poor shepherd *treated* him *with* great kindness.

He was accused of *treating with* the enemy during a war.

treat *of:* (usually in a scholarly context) This article *treats of* the three types of argumentation.

treat *for:* The doctor *treated* him *for* measles, chicken pox, and scarlet fever all at once.

treat *to:* I *treated* my entire family *to* a double-dip rocky-road icecream cone.

Below is a list of idiomatic phrases containing prepositions which are commonly the source of mistakes. Read through the list to make yourself more aware of these words. However, do not try to memorize such lists. Become familiar with their use by listening, talking, and reading.

accordance with:	in accordance with company policy
accountable for:	accountable for her own conduct
accountable to:	accountable to no one but himself
acquiesce in:	acquiesce in a plan to execute the dictator
acquit of:	acquitted of all misdemeanor charges
adhere to:	adhered to the strictest rules of conduct
analogous to:	analogous to a spaceship
analogy with:	his analogy of earth with a spaceship
aspire to:	aspires to the Presidency
attribute to:	abnormal behavior which can be attributed to brain damage
characteristic of:	characteristic of those who have hardening of the arteries
charge with:	charged with murder; charged with safekeeping the company's records

compatible with:	a policy not compatible with the aim of world peace
concerned about:	concerned about her poor health
concerned for:	concerned for the innocent victims
concerned with:	a matter concerned with the use of our funds
concerns himself with:	concerns himself with the affairs of others
concur in:	to concur in this decision
concur with:	the U.S. concurring with the British on this issue
consistent with:	behavior consistent with his past record
contribute to:	contribute to the eradication of disease
deprived of:	deprived of home and security
different from:	different from the previous ruler
distinct from:	"enjoyment" as distinct from "happiness"
distinguish between:	distinguish between the laws of science and the laws of ethics
distinguish from:	distinguish these laws from those laws
divide between:	money divided *between* his aunt and his niece, money divided *among* his five nephews. (However, *between* is occasionally used for more than two, especially in informal situations.)
endowed with:	endowed with a million dollars
implicit in:	consent not given in so many words but implicit in his remarks about personal responsibility
implied by:	consent implied by his remarks
inconsistent with:	a philosophy inconsistent with controls
infer from:	can infer from her speech that she opposes such freedom
liable for:	liable for medical claims that may be brought against her
liable to:	(informal for *likely to*)
objective of:	objective of the mission

peculiar to:	a custom peculiar to this religious sect
pertinent to:	laws not pertinent to juvenile crime
prohibit from:	prohibited from trespassing
succeeded in	
(or succeeded at):	succeeded in guessing his name
succeeded to:	succeeded to the throne
tendency to:	tendency to become violent
tendency toward:	tendency toward laziness

Pairs of Words Commonly Confused

Use this list in the way most helpful to you. Consult particular words when directed to do so. If you are already quite confident with words, then read through the list to make sure you are aware of all of these distinctions.

An asterisk (*) is used to show incorrect usage.

accept/except
>   *Accept* is the verb: She *accepted* the honor.
>   *Except* is the preposition akin to *exception: Except* for Harry, everyone was there. With the *exception* of Harry, everyone was there.

advice/advise
>   *Advice* is the noun: They give *advice.*
>   *Advise* is the verb: They have *advised* me to . . .

affect/effect
>   *Affect* is a verb: Will the drug *affect* his mind?
>   *Effect,* akin to *effective,* is usually a noun: We could see no such *effect.*
>   *Effect* can sometimes be a verb: The committee wants to *effect* (bring about) change.

all ready/already
>   *All ready* means '' all prepared'': The men are *all ready* to go.
>   *Already* refers to time: They are *already* briefed. They are *already* dressed.

all together/altogether

All together means "all in a group."

Altogether means "completely": They are *altogether* unreliable.

allusion/illusion/delusion/elusive

Allusion means "reference": His *allusion to* Christ . . . He *alluded to* Christ.

Illusion, like "hallucination" or "dream" refers to something not really in existence or not really true: The apparent curve was an optical *illusion.*

Delusion: If one is really deceived by a false impression, he is *deluded* by it; the false belief is a *delusion.*

Elusive suggests something hard to catch, almost slippery: The criminal was *elusive; he eluded* all attempts at capture. The truth was *elusive.*

amount/number (less/fewer)

Amount is used with mass nouns like "sugar" or "flour": a small *amount of sugar*

Number is used with count nouns like "people" and "countries": "Countries" can be counted, but "flour" and "sugar" cannot. Thus a *number of people* but not *a large amount of people,* nor *a large amount of countries.*

Less and *fewer* observe the same restrictions. *Less* is restricted to mass nouns: *less food, less water, less sympathy.* Such phrases as *less people, less countries* are not allowed. Count nouns require the word *fewer: fewer people* and *fewer countries.*

(Notice that *more* applies to both count nouns and mass nouns: *more people, more sugar, more sympathy,* and *more countries.*)

approve of/approve

Approve of refers to personal attitudes about something: I *approve of* her choice.

Approve means to give official ratification: A President might approve a treaty, although he previously disapproved of it.

attribute/contribute

Attribute: One *attributes* an effect *to* a cause; e.g., We can

attribute this broken window *to* last night's vandalism.
Contribute can mean "to cause" or "be part of a cause": Rising costs *contributed to* the discomfort of the middle class.

choose/chose

Frequently a spelling mistake. *Chose,* which rhymes with *froze,* is the past tense of *choose.*

cite/sight/site

Cite often means "set forth": to *cite* evidence, *cite* statistics, *cite* your own experience
Sight is the common word akin to *seeing.*
Site means "place."

complement/compliment

Complement is related to "complete." Together, two things complement each other or make a whole: Bare wooden timbers in a room *complement* rough-textured walls. Two jobs can *complement* each other.
Compliment is related to "praise."

conscience/conscious

Conscience is the individual's knowledge of what is right and wrong.
Conscious means "aware" or "awake."

continual/continuous

Continual means happening repeatedly over a period of time: The phone rings *continually.*
Continuous suggests that there is no stopping and starting: The water ran *continuously.*

council/counsel/consul

A *council* is a group of committee, like the President's *Council* on Economic Affairs.
Counsel is advice. He gave good *counsel.*
A *consul* is an official, who often lives in a foreign city to look after the commercial interests of the home country.

credible/credulous/creditable

Credible means "believable." I found his story *credible*.

Credulous applies to a person in a believing frame of mind, though not necessarily "gullible."

Creditable applies to behavior which reflects credit on the persons involved.

disinterested/uninterested

Disinterested is an appropriate attitude—impartial and unbiassed: Only disinterested persons may serve on juries.

Uninterested refers to "lack of interest."

due to/because of

Because of is favored by professional writers.

Due to is more often found in bureaucratic prose and carries with it a bureaucratic flavor.

formally/formerly

Formally means "in a formal way."

Formerly refers to the past. He was *formerly* a senator but is now an ambassador.

human/humane

Human refers to people as opposed to animals

Humane suggests decency and compassion: It was a *humane* act.

imply/infer

Imply is what a writer does when he communicates meaning but not in an explicit way: He *implied* that I was a liar, even if he didn't say so.

Infer is what the reader does when he puts two and two together as he reads. His inferences or conclusions may or may not be justified, of course: I *inferred* from his letter that he was coming to meet me.

irrelevant/irreverent

Irrelevant means "not pertinent": This data is irrelevant.

Irreverent suggests disrespect.

its/it's
> *Its* is possessive: The cat drank *its* milk.
> *It's* is the contraction for "it is" or "it has."

judicial/judicious
> *Judicial* refers to judges, courts, and laws.
> *Judicious* suggests "wise," "prudent," or "cautious."

lead/led
> Frequently confused. *Lead,* when it rhymes with *led,* means the kind of *lead* in a pencil. The past tense of the verb *to lead* is spelled *led.*

lie/lay
> *Lie* means "to recline." She *lies down* after lunch every day.
> *Lay* is the past tense of "lie." She *lay down* after lunch, but now she's up again.
> *Lay,* in another sense, means "to put." Will you *lay* this on the table? I *laid* it on the table yesterday.

lose/loose
> A frequent spelling mistake. *Lose* is pronounced "looze."
> *Loose* is pronounced with a hissing *s.*

luxurious/luxuriant
> *Luxurious* is what new homes might be called: A *luxurious* home in an affluent suburb.
> *Luxuriant* means "thick" or "abundant" usually, but not always, in connection with plants: The *luxuriant* vegetation and the closeness of the air were almost unpleasant.

moral/morale
> *Moral* refers to right and wrong: He considered it a *moral* obligation.
> *Morale* means "spirit" or "mood": the *morale* of the troops.

practical/practicable
> *Practical* is the opposite of theoretical: He was a brilliant man

but not very *practical.*

Practicable means "can be done" or "feasible:" They claimed
that mass transit was no longer *practicable.*

proceed/precede

Proceed means "go ahead": *Proceed* with the plan.

Precede means "to go in front of": The captain *preceded* his
troops into battle. Mr. Gray *preceded* me in this job.

principle/principal

Principle means "rule:" He knew the *principle* of navigation.

Principal is the "chief" or "main" part of something: She was
the *principal* source of ideas.

prophecy/prophesy

Prophecy is the noun: All were alarmed by his *prophecy.*

Prophesy (the last syllable rhymes with "pie") is the verb: He
was able to *prophesy* the coming of the Messiah.

respectfully/respectively

Respectfully means "in a respectful manner."

Respectively is used to show relationships or connections:
Seated left to right are Smith, Brown, and Gomez, the President, Vice-President, and Treasurer, *respectively.*

there/their

There refers to place.

Their is the possessive of *them: Their* ideas, *their* responsibility.

whose/who's

Whose is the possessive of *who:* I've discovered a writer *whose*
ideas are exciting and novel.

Who's means *who is* or *who has: Who's* coming now? *Who's*
arrived lately?

Mistakes with Metaphor

Writers using metaphors sometimes produce visual confusions of
the kind illustrated here. The remedy lies first in being able to spot

the confusion, and second in being able to rephrase the sentence.

This student writer compares the Constitution to the foundation of a building:

> They laid down the foundation of the federal government under the Constitution. The Constitution was the foundation by which men consented to govern themselves.

First, the Constitution is a structure resting on some foundation, and then it is the foundation itself. And how do men govern themselves by a foundation? One possible rephrasing is this one:

> The Constitution was to be the foundation for the new federal government. It was the set of principles by which the citizens would govern themselves.

An extreme example like this one:

> The key to the solution, if we can unravel it, will dissolve all doubts.

is beyond repair. The writer may be suggesting that there is one solution, and only one, and once this solution is discovered everyone will recognize it as the correct solution. If we accept such a statement, we must still recognize that it tells us very little. Moreover, one should not need to be a Sherlock Holmes to work out what the writer means. Metaphors are meant to make meaning clearer, not to conceal it.

Clichés

Phrases like "in a nutshell," "well-rounded person" and "the American way of life" are ready-made metaphorical phrases. Such phrases are called *clichés* after an old printer's instrument. In an unthinking, mechanical way a writer can reproduce stock phrases in the same way that a printer could stamp an entire word or phrase on a sheet of paper—no trouble, no thinking, no originality involved. Unfortunately, the phrases communicate this staleness, lack of force, and evidence of shallowness to the reader.

Phrases like the following are typical:

building blocks of success	life is not a bowl of cherries
through thick and thin	(or bed of roses)
all walks of life	a ray of hope
taking the bull by the horns	

One problem with giving advice about clichés is that certain of them have become so embedded in the language that avoiding them may lead to more awkwardness than using them. When used in appropriate contexts "the tide turned," "(someone's) back to the wall," or "face to face" may be more communicative than paraphrases.

Certain ideas can be clichés, the ideas for example that the savage is childlike, that businessmen have ulcers, that women long to be mothers, that Scotsmen are penny-pinchers, that success comes to those who work hard. This is not to imply that such ideas are never true. They may indeed be true. The fault is to utter such notions when they are divorced from experience or data.

For example, the writer of the following introduction to a paper on modern art appears not to have thought beyond conventional and expected clichés about the subject:

> One of our modern problems of society is that in this world of white, middle-class values a person with unconventional ideas who is a little different is looked down on. You are not accepted unless you are a conformist. This is why modern art is not popular today.

A more determined and original approach to the subject might include a more detailed account of the "white, middle-class values" as contrasted with the values suggested by particular works of modern art. As it is, the writer's first paragraph provides little hope that he will say much of interest, drawn from his individual experience. This is the main problem with cliché—its use is likely to shut off genuine and productive communication.

Written Slang

Written slang, like its spoken counterpart, is a vigorous kind of language used in very informal situations. Personal letters to friends are the most obvious places where slang may be appropriate; it is almost never used in legal briefs, formal correspondence, or in academic writing.

Most readers would judge it inappropriate for someone to write on a job application:

> My credentials and qualifications are *pretty heavy* [i.e., *impressive*].

or to write in an academic report:

> Reports by Miller, 1967, and Harrison, 1972, suggest that such attempts at peer group identification are not *genuinely cool.*

Colloquial English

There are many kinds of written English, ranging from the sometimes stilted English of a presidential address to the everyday slang just discussed. Written English is a very conservative medium. The use of colloquial expressions in a piece of writing communicates an informal conversational manner. Such a manner is rarely appropriate for academic writing where formality is often regarded as showing seriousness and informality is interpreted as revealing either frivolity or a lack of sensitivity to what is appropriate. Expressions like *fire* meaning ''dismiss,'' *be floored* (by a problem), *fix* meaning ''prepare food'' are usually labeled as colloquialisms. If you are unsure about a particular expression, a large dictionary is a useful guide, although its use of the term *colloquialism* is likely to include slang and many clichés. Unfortunately what is colloquial for one reader may be quite acceptable to another equally scholarly person. You have considerable scope for your own judgment as to the suitability of language for the topic and audience.

Wordiness

Say simply and directly what you want to say. Scratch out words which add nothing to the meaning. A wordy sentence like this one:

> They all bear a distinct similarity in the fact that they are eloquent.

can be changed to a shorter one:

> They are all eloquent.

Not only does the writer save words and space, but he gains in forcefulness.

> If we look at the whole situation logically, we see a problem. For every problem there is a solution. In order for something to be solved, it must answer the problem in such a fashion that there are no other problems created. The problem of student demonstrations is a deep, involved problem, yet there is a solution. The solution does not lie with arresting or expelling. Where it hides is a secret not yet told.

A reduced version is better, clearer, and more forceful:

> Arresting or expelling those who participate in demonstrations will not solve the complex problem of student unrest.

It is useful to divide Wordiness into three categories.

Wordiness I, the most annoying, is the most long-winded, pretentious, or pompous. The writer appears not to have thought out what he wants to say. He has nothing very specific to say, and he thinks in great cloudy generalities. The rambling passage on student unrest is feeble.

Wordiness 2 (Redundancy) is less severe, less annoying. The writer has accidentally said the same thing twice or more.

> Violent death has now become a commonplace thing, a thing of everyday occurrence in life.

The remedy is to scratch out the unnecessary phrases so that the sentence reads

Better: Violent death has now become commonplace.

Occasionally, one idea is implied by an earlier one. Again, delete the unnecessary word.

It was gray *in appearance.*

could just as well be

It was gray.

since the word *gray* implies *in appearance.*

Wordiness 3 involves single words which should frequently be eliminated. Note the examples:

War is regarded as (being) brave, righteous, and honorable.

To a Benedictine monk (obtaining) peace of mind is not gained by reaching out and acquiring all the things that laymen crave.

EXERCISE

How could the following be rephrased to eliminate stuffy, wordy, pompous, and pretentious prose? For example, here is one way you can rephrase the first sentence:

One difference is the student coach in English classes here. At Scarborough High School English classes do not have coaches.

1. One of the differences between the English classes in this school and those of Scarborough High School is that of a student coach in this school.
2. According to the author, it is obvious to him that military games and toys should be discontinued entirely.
3. Writer Y perceives that the selfish character of man and the nature of the earth make the institution of war an unending process and one which will continue as long as man exists.

4. We can, through generalizing the nature of the problem, see that the trouble appears to lie in our inability to grasp relationships.

5. This necessary effort is essential for the safety of the school children.

6. At a glance one can tell that these writers are of completely opposite differences of opinion.

7. The opening of the tape is more or less an introduction to prepare the listener for what is to come. It mostly says to have an open mind for what is to come. This opening is a song, "Listen," which informs the audience that it is important to listen and be aware.

8. But what I think is true is that because children are supposed to be so controlled with their releases that when the point comes to where they are supposed to give in to their impulses, the strain of the withholding will create guilt subterfuges, and situations which might have been avoided.

9. One has to be sure about beginning skiing because the cost of equipment is quite expensive.

10. I have not learned anything of value from these movies that will benefit me in the future.

11. Science, in its never-ending search for answers, continually demands new and innovative methods for solving the problems which constantly confront them.

Mechanics

Abbreviations

In special kinds of written forms such as legal documents, technical papers, footnotes, and addresses on post cards, abbreviations are used to save time and space. Since there is little need for that kind of economy in college writing, however, abbreviations should generally be avoided. Use abbreviations only when you think they will help the reader.

TITLES

Write out all titles except Mr., Messrs., Mrs., Mmes., Ms., St., and Dr. If these titles are not followed by a proper name they too should be written out.

Incorrect: The Dr. was sued for malpractice.

Correct: Dr. Fry (or *The doctor*) was sued for malpractice.

171

Certain titles like Reverend, the Honorable, Colonel, President, are usually written out. They can be abbreviated only if the first name or initials are included.

Incorrect: Rev. Hayes, Hon. Blake.

Correct: Rev. Christopher Hayes, Hon. D. R. Blake.

DEGREES

Academic degrees are usually abbreviated: B.A., M.A., Ph.D., M.D., D.D.S. Use a title either before *or* after the name, but not both places.

Incorrect: Dr. J. W. Myer, Ph.D.

Correct: Dr. J. W. Myer, or J. W. Myer, Ph.D.

COUNTRIES, STATES, ETC.

Spell out names of countries, states, months, days of the week, and units of measure.

Incorrect: Victoria lost six lbs. between Mon. and Fri.

Correct: Victoria lost six pounds between Monday and Friday.

In general writing, spell out words like *Avenue, Boulevard,* and *Company.*

Correct: Gunn's Trailer Company is situated between Claremont Road and Wyoming Boulevard.

FAMILIAR ABBREVIATIONS

You may use familiar abbreviations for organizations, government agencies, trade names, scientific words, and technical terms.

CIA	Central Intelligence Agency
ROTC	Reserve Officer Training Corps
RNA	Ribonucleic acid
Rh factor	Rhesus factor
OED	Oxford English Dictionary

UNFAMILIAR ABBREVIATIONS

If you plan to use repeatedly an abbreviation that is not commonly known, explain it the first time you use it.

> Stop Littering Our Bays and Beaches, an organization commonly known to San Diego residents as SLOBB, sent out fifty members to clean the Solana Beach coastline.

LATIN EXPRESSIONS

Commonly known Latin expressions may be used in abbreviated form, though many writers prefer to use the English equivalents.

cf.	*confer* means *compare*
e.g.	*exempli grata* means *for example*
i.e.	*id est* means *that is*
etc.	*et cetera* means *and so forth*

(NOTE: In general *etc.* should be avoided in college writing. Rephrase your list, introducing it with *such as* or *including*. The literal translation *and so forth* is only a little better than *etc.*)

Inappropriate: The intramural program consists of baseball, basketball, swimming, golf, etc.

Appropriate: The intramural program consists of sports such as baseball, basketball, swimming, and golf.

Appropriate: The intramural program includes baseball, basketball, swimming, and golf.

(NOTE: If an abbreviation comes at the end of a sentence, only one period is used.)

> Plato, the Greek philosopher, died in 347 A.D.

Agreement

SUBJECT AND VERB

Singular subjects require singular verbs; plural subjects require plural verbs.

> The baker decorates the cake.
> The bakers decorate_ the cake.

INTERVENING PHRASE. When the subject is followed immediately by the verb, as in the above examples, mistakes in agreement are rarely made. When there is an intervening phrase, however, some writers may make the verb agree with the nearest noun, rather than with the actual subject of the sentence.

> Gardiner, together with a number of less well-known associates, has formed a powerful and highly independent public lobby. (*Gardiner has,* not *a number have*)

> The bogus manuscripts, whose lack of authenticity was discovered by William Day, make interesting reading nevertheless. (*Manuscripts make,* not *William Day makes*)

INVERTED SENTENCE. When the word order of a sentence is inverted, agreement is sometimes difficult to establish. Be sure to identify the true subject of the sentence correctly, especially if it comes after the verb.

> Riding the horse were the two girls, Valerie and Therese. (*girls were,* not *horse was*)

> In the greenhouse grow many varieties of flowers. (*varieties grow,* not *greenhouse grows*)

COMPOUND SUBJECT. Two or more subjects joined by *and* take a plural verb.

> Karate and judo *seem* to be increasing in popularity.

> Rushing the passer and covering punts are the major deficiencies in the Chargers' defense.

(NOTE: When a compound subject refers to a single thing, the verb is singular.)

> Blood, Sweat & Tears appeals to many age groups because of its effective combination of rock and jazz.

COMPOUND SUBJECT: *OR, NOR.* If two or more subjects are joined by *or, nor, either . . . or,* or *neither . . . nor,* the verb should agree with the nearer subject.

> Neither oils nor *water colors have* been purchased by the Art Department.

> Either the dogs or the *cat has* to go.

> Either the dog or the *cats have* to go.

COLLECTIVE NOUNS.

1. A singular verb is used when the collective noun is regarded as a unit.

   > The *cast* of *Waiting for Godot is* a small one.

   > The archaeology *section is* planning a dig near Poway this summer.

2. A plural verb is used if the collective noun refers to the members of the group.

   > The *cast* of *Waiting for Godot* continually *miss* their cues.

   > The archaeology *section,* sitting apart from the rest, *were* drinking their chocolate milk and balancing their tuna sandwiches on their knees.

(NOTE: The last examples, though grammatically correct, have an awkward sound to them. For these and like sentences, it is often better to use a subject that is clearly plural.)

> The members of the cast of *Waiting for Godot* continually miss their cues.

> The archaeologists sat apart from the rest, drinking their chocolate milk and balancing their tuna sandwiches on their knees.

PRONOUNS AS SUBJECTS. Note that the following pronouns are singular and therefore require singular verbs:

anybody	everybody	somebody	either	one
anyone	everyone	someone	neither	none
anything	everything	something	each	nobody

We believe that everyone who *has* visited this exhibit *has* left with a deeper understanding of urban problems.

Neither poet *writes* about the individual in crisis.

But although some purists insist that *none* can only be singular, the word is widely used as a plural:

None of the writers *has* captured the immigrant experience as eloquently as Elia Kazan.

None of the writers *have* captured the immigrant experience as eloquently as Elia Kazan.

NOUNS PLURAL IN FORM BUT SINGULAR IN MEANING. Though a few nouns appear to be plural because they end in *s,* their meaning makes them singular. They take singular verbs.

Rabies is always fatal if not treated immediately.

Mathematics is required of all freshmen.

Economics has been added to the curriculum of the graduate school.

EXPLETIVES: *THERE IS, THERE ARE, IT IS.* A sentence may begin with the expletive or introductory word *there* (sometimes called an ''anticipating subject''). Whether the verb is singular or plural depends on the subject which follows the expletive.

There *are* numerous *cases* of heroin overdose not only in the inner city, but in the suburbs as well.

In my opinion, there *is* little *evidence* of criminal intent.

It always takes the singular *is,* even if a following noun is plural:

It is the mountains which I find so difficult to sketch.

SHIFTS IN TENSE AND PERSON

VERBS. Avoid needless and confusing shifts of tenses.

Shift: Mill *stresses* the importance of originality as the catalyst for social progress and *insisted* that individuality must not be repressed.

Consistent: Mill *stresses* . . . and *insists*. . . .

Consistent: Mill *stressed* . . . and *insisted*. . . .

Shift: For months I *had admired* Susan Morange from afar, but I *haven't* the courage to ask her for a date.

Consistent: For months I *had admired* . . . but I *hadn't*. . . .

Consistent: For months I *have admired* . . . but I *haven't*. . . .

PRONOUNS (PERSON OF). Avoid needless and confusing shifts of pronouns from one person to another. (First person: *I, we;* second person: *you;* third person: *he, she, it, one, they.*)

Shift: If *one* is to read Beckett's plays intelligently, *you* should first familiarize *yourself* with Beckett's novels. (A shift from third to second person.)

Consistent: If *one* is to read Beckett's plays intelligently, *he* should first familiarize *himself* with Beckett's novels.

Consistent: If you are to read Beckett's plays intelligently, *you* should first familiarize *yourself* with Beckett's novels.

Students often are in a quandary about the use of the first person *I* in a paper. There should be no hesitancy to use *I* if the paper concerns a personal experience. However, if the paper is of a more general nature—comparing the outlooks of two historians, for example—the first person should be used sparingly. Because the student is expressing his own opinions, the *I* in such a paper is taken for granted even though it doesn't actually appear. To make the *I* explicit in such a sentence as "*I believe* Marx criticized the Industrial Revolution in his early works" is a waste of words. If there is an instance, however, when the writer makes a point contrary to someone else's, the use of *I* is vastly preferable to such tortured phrases as "This writer thinks" or "The author of this paper believes." In short, when a reference to yourself is necessary, feel free to use *I*.

PRONOUN AND ANTECEDENT

A pronoun should agree in number with its antecedent. A singular antecedent requires a singular pronoun; a plural antecedent requires a plural pronoun.

> *John* felt *he* deserved a raise.
>
> The *employees* felt *they* deserved raises.

INTERVENING PHRASE.   Mistakes in agreement generally occur when the pronoun is separated from its antecedent by an intervening phrase. Be sure to identify the correct antecedent.

> It is all too easy to get lost inside a complex sentence and to make grammatical *errors* which won't seem obvious at a *glance* but *which* impedes comprehension.

The relative pronoun *which* refers to "errors," not "glance," so the "which" is plural, not singular. Hence it takes the verb "impede," not "impedes."

ANTECEDENTS: COMPOUND NOUNS.   A pronoun referring to compound nouns joined by *and* is usually plural.

> Even though *Chris* and *Tim* were expert swimmers, *they* were drowned in a dangerous rip tide.
>
> *Chris* and *Tim* lost *their* lives.

A pronoun referring to compound nouns joined by *or, nor, either . . . or,* or *neither . . . nor* usually agrees with the nearer antecedent.

She took advantage of anyone or *anything which* could further her career.

She took advantage of anything or *anyone who* could further her career.

In sentences like the following, however, the plural pronoun is customary even when the second noun of the subject is singular:

Neither the father nor the sons have finished *their* household chores.

Neither the sons nor the father have finished *their* household chores.

ANTECEDENTS: COLLECTIVE NOUNS. A collective noun takes a singular pronoun if the noun is regarded as a unit.

The *jury* took *its* time in reaching a decision.

A collective noun takes a plural pronoun if the noun refers to the members of the group.

Deciding that *they* could reach no decision that night, the *jury* retired to *their* rooms to get some sleep.

(NOTE: To avoid awkwardness, it is sometimes better to add a subject that is clearly plural.)

The members of the jury, the jury members.

Deciding that they could reach no decision that night, *the jury members* retired to their rooms to get some sleep.

PRONOUN FORMS: WHO *OR* WHOM, I *OR* ME

WHO, WHOM. *Who* and *whoever* are normally subjects. *Whom* and *whomever* are objects of verbs or of prepositions.

Whoever arrives first should make the first speech.

It is irrelevant *who* did the damage.

Present the bill to *whoever* broke the window. (*Whoever* is the subject of its own clause.)

To *whom* did you give such poor advice?

Chisholm was the candidate *whom* we most admired.

(NOTE: *That* is also possible in the last example while *who* is increasingly acceptable.)

CLAUSES. When a pronoun is a subject of a clause, it takes the subject form even when the whole clause is the object of a verb or of a preposition.

Give this to *whoever* is wearing a red carnation. (*Whoever* is the subject of the clause *whoever is wearing a red carnation.*)

I condemn only those *who* are unwilling to forgive. (*Who* is the subject of the clause *who are unwilling to forgive.*)

AFTER PREPOSITIONS. Pronouns which follow prepositions take the object form.

He showed the experiment to *me*.

Mr. Szanto will probably divide the work between you and *me*.

APPOSITIVES. An appositive should be in the same case as the noun or pronoun it explains.

We, Bart and *I*, went to the Del Mar Racetrack.

The foreman shouted at both of us, Pete and *me*, before we had a chance to explain.

Capitals

There are two fundamental rules to remember: Capitalize the first word of a sentence. Capitalize proper nouns and adjectives.

Here are some other guidelines.

SENTENCES AND POETRY

1. Capitalize the first word of a sentence.
2. Capitalize the first word of each line of poetry when the poem is printed in the traditional way.

> Wind, bird, and tree,
> Water, grass, and light:
> In half of what I write
> Roughly or smoothly
> Year by impatient year,
> The same six words recur.
> —David Wagoner, ''The Words''

3. Capitalize the first word of a direct quotation that is a complete sentence in itself.

> Stan Mason says, ''The finest automobile built today is the Ferrari.''

No capital is used if the quotation is a fragment.

> Stan Mason claims that he was ''financially embarrassed.''

4. Capitalize the first word after a colon only when the statement that follows the colon is lengthy or when you want to give the statement particular emphasis. When in doubt, use the lower case.

WORDS THAT ARE CAPITALIZED

1. The personal pronoun *I* and the exclamation *O*.
2. Words referring to the Deity and Holy Scripture.

> the Lord   the Koran
> the New Testament   the power of His love

3. Days of the week, names of months, and calendar items. Names of seasons are *not* capitalized.

> Tuesday   Labor Day
> February   winter

4. Official titles before (not after) the name of the bearer.

He visited Governor Rockefeller.

He visited Nelson Rockefeller, governor of our state.

5. Proper names of persons, places, and things, but not names of classes of persons, places, and things.

Capitalize	*Do not capitalize*
Sam	a man
Mr. Jones	a man
Florida	a southern state
People's Park	a park
Sather Gate	a monument
Notre Dame University	a midwest university
2815 Los Arboles Court	a shady street
Literature 2B	a literature course

(NOTE: The Junior Prom, but, Jerry is a junior.)

6. Religious, racial, linguistic, national, and political groups.

Catholic	Polynesian	Communist
Negro	French	Spanish

(NOTE: At this point in history many writers capitalize *Black* just as they capitalize *Spanish* and *English.*)

7. Names of social and economic groups are not capitalized.

the bourgeoisie   the aristocracy

8. Names denoting family relationships are capitalized when used with the person's name or when they stand for the name. They are not capitalized when preceded by a possessive.

My first mitt was given to me by Grandpa Brown.

My first mitt was given to me by Grandpa.

My first mitt was given to me by my grandpa.

9. Historical periods or events.

the Iron Age   the Battle of Algiers

10. North, south, east, and west are capitalized only if they refer to a specific location.

I was born in the Southwest.

The map says we should travel further south.

11. In titles of books, articles, papers, and the like, capitalize the first and last word, important words, and prepositions of more than four letters. Do not capitalize articles (*a, an, the*) or conjunctions.

King Kong Meets the Daughter of Frankenstein

"Casey at the Bat"

"My Life Before and After the War"

12. Names of trains, aircraft, and ships.

Hyphens

The hyphen is most often used to link two or more words which are considered as a single unit. However there is a growing tendency, especially with two-word combinations, to omit the hyphen and to write the combination as a single word. Moreover two-word combinations appear to go through three major stages—at first as nouns they appear as two separate words without a hyphen, as did *rail road;* then as adjectives preceding a noun as a hyphenated combination, *rail-road;* and finally, some years after they become assimilated into common vocabulary, as a single word, *railroad*. Thus, we cannot give a set of cast-iron rules for inserting or omitting hyphens; we can only set some guidelines. For specific words, consult the most recent edition of a good dictionary.

1. Use a hyphen between two words used as a single adjective *in front* of a noun, as in

>   The *well-known* playwright arrived in a *reddish-brown* convertible with a *freckle-faced, red-haired* child.

   However, if the combination *follows* the noun, the hyphen is usually omitted:

>   The playwright was *well known*.
>
>   The convertible was *reddish brown*.
>
>   The child was *freckle faced* and *red haired*.

   The hyphen is also omitted if the first part of the combination is an *-ly* adverb, as in

>   the gently swaying trees
>
>   the irritatingly arrogant monarch

2. Use hyphens for other word combinations considered as a single unit, such as

>   mother-in-law
>   great-grandfather
>   able-bodied
>   letter-perfect

3. Use a hyphen after such prefixes as *pro-, ex-,* and *self-,* as in

pro-consul
ex-convict
self-made man

Here again there is considerable variation. For example, *pre-meditated* and *prehistoric* no longer have hyphens while *pre-industrial* still requires one.

4. Where a prefix ending in a vowel is combined with a word beginning with a vowel, a hyphen usually appears, as in

re-engage
anti-establishment

There is considerable variation for words beginning with *co-*.

co-worker	cooperate
co-exist	coexist
co-conspirator	coincidence

5. Use a hyphen between prefixes and proper names.

pre-Christian
anti-American (but *antisocial*)
pro-Italian

6. Use a hyphen to prevent confusing one word with another word with the same spelling, such as

recreation	*and*	re-creation
resort	*and*	re-sort
recover	*and*	re-cover

7. Use a hyphen to separate written-out numbers *twenty-one* through *ninety-nine,* and to separate written-out fractions such as *three-eighths.* However, you may omit a hyphen from commonly used fractions such as *one half* and *two thirds.*

8. Use a hyphen to break words at the end of a line. See *Word Division.*

Italics

Where a printer uses italics, the typist uses underlining. The *New York Times* is the same as the New York Times. The following should be underlined in your writing:

1. Underline titles of books, magazines, plays, motion pictures, operas, long poems, and works of art.

> The Scarlet Letter   (novel)
> Time   (magazine)
> Who's Afraid of Virginia Woolf   (play)
> Godzilla Meets Dracula   (movie)
> La Bohème   (opera)
> Paradise Lost   (long poem)
> The Thinker   (statue)

Do *not* underline titles of magazine or newspaper articles, songs, poems, or short stories.

> "The Snows of Kilimanjaro" by Hemingway
> "Alcoholism in America," reprinted in the Chicago Sun Times

2. Underline words referred to as words.

> I notice in your paper you misspelled expedient twice. (You may use quotation marks instead of underlining.)

3. Underline names of ships, trains, and aircraft.
4. Underline scientific names.

> ursus terribilis   (grizzly bear)

5. Underline foreign phrases not yet naturalized into English. Refer to your dictionary to see which words are still thought of as foreign.

> quantum libet   (as much as you please)
> post cibum   (after meals)
> post facto   (after the fact)

There is no need to underline a foreign expression if it is in quotation marks. You must underline, however, if foreign and English words are mixed.

"Lo meteremos en un colegio," said Pablo.

"You are his sister, n'est-ce pas?" he asked.

Be sure to underline abbreviations of Latin words in footnotes such as ibid., op. cit.

UNDERLINING FOR EMPHASIS

Underlining is a crude way to show emphasis in expository writing. Instead of

Armando Rodriguez argued that difference is strength, not destruction.

one can write

It was Armando Rodriguez who argued that difference is strength, not destruction.

or

Armando Rodriguez was the man who argued that difference is strength, not destruction.

But underlining is often used to good effect in the writing of dialogue because it accentuates the speaker's inflection and gives us insight into the speaker's character.

"I introduce him to all my friends. Let him clutter up the whole apartment with his horrible manuscript papers, and cigarette butts, and radishes, and what not."—J. D. Salinger, "Just Before the War with the Eskimos."

Numbers

The main question regarding numbers is whether to use only the figure or whether to write out the word. These rules describe the customary use of numbers.

WHEN TO USE WORDS TO REPRESENT NUMBERS

1. Isolated numbers under 100.

> I saw four killer whales.

(NOTE: In a series of numbers of which some are less than 100 and others more, be consistent. Normally you should use figures.)

> I saw 4 killer whales, 8 lady bugs, 13 giraffes, and 152 aardvarks.

2. Numbers at the beginning of sentences.

> Three hundred and eleven Cub Scouts attended the Jamboree.

(NOTE: Dates are an exception to this rule.)

> 1963 was a good year for Amalgamated Hinges.

3. Round numbers or indefinite expressions.

> I've told you a million times not to exaggerate!

> The Beatles drew forty or fifty thousand to their concert at Shea Stadium.

WHEN TO USE FIGURES TO REPRESENT NUMBERS

1. Most writers continue to write out numbers from one to a hundred. It is acceptable, however, to use figures for numbers of 10 or more.

> There are 43 more than expected.

> There are forty-three more than expected.

> There are 542 more than expected.

2. Dates.

> September 21, 1944

> She lived in Baltimore from August 5, 1938 to June 7, 1963.

(NOTE: Always write out in full the ordinal form for the day of the month: fifth, third, ninth.)

3. Street, room, and telephone numbers.

    Send my mail to 2354 North Sierra, Solana Beach, California, 92075.

4. Measurements.

    Please use $8\frac{1}{2}$ by 11 paper for your assignments.

    The carton weighed 22 pounds, 11 ounces.

5. Money.

    $3.24, $18 apiece, $0.44, 44 cents.

6. Decimals and percentages.

    She owed 42 percent of the bill.

    The pole measured 42.8 feet.

7. Time of day when used with A.M. or P.M.

    8:00 A.M., eight o'clock

8. Pages and divisions of a book.

    p. 4, Chapter 9, pp. 6–11, Act V, Scene II, line 29.

9. Use commas to separate the thousands from the hundreds. This is optional for round numbers.

    2500 or 2,500; 4,311,248.

CARDINAL AND ORDINAL NUMBERS

Cardinal numbers indicate number only: 2, 3, 19.

Ordinal numbers indicate order: second, third, nineteenth. Ordinal numbers should not be abbreviated (2nd, 3rd, 19th) but written out.

PLURALS OF NUMBERS

Plurals of numbers are written either with *'s* or *s:*

I need four 2 by 4's. (2 by 4s)

In your list, I notice only three 6's (6s) and two 12's (12s).

Parallelism

When comparing or contrasting one thing with another within a sentence, or when using a series of words or phrases, express the relationship in a parallel grammatical structure. The rule for constructing parallel forms is a simple one: express similar ideas in similar forms. Match nouns with nouns, verbs with verbs, infinitives with infinitives, prepositional phrases with prepositional phrases. If you mix constructions, the relationship between ideas is obscured, and the reader might be confused.

Some violations of parallel structure may not cause real misunderstanding:

Steak and lobster are my favorite foods, and so is eating chicken.

But the following parallel sentence sounds better and makes more sense:

Steaks, lobster, and chicken are my favorite foods.

Sentences which lack parallelism can be corrected in more than one way. Whichever grammatical construction you choose for your sentence, however, remember to use it consistently.

Not Parallel: Early to bed and rising early makes a man healthy, gives him wealth, and he will be wise.

Parallel: Early to bed and early to rise gives a man health, wealth, and wisdom.

Parallel: If a man goes to bed early and rises early, he will be healthy, wealthy, and wise.

Parallel: Early to bed and early to rise makes a man healthy, wealthy, and wise.

Parallel: Going to bed early and getting up early makes a man healthy, wealthy, and wise.

SERIES

Use a parallel construction to express a series of words, phrases or clauses.

Not Parallel: Automobile manufacturers are alleged to have tried to spy on critics to conceal safety data, to restrain competition, and buying off influential legislators.

Parallel: Automobile manufacturers are alleged to have tried to spy on critics, to conceal safety data, to restrain competition, and to buy off influential legislators.

Parallel: Automobile manufacturers are alleged to have tried spying on critics, concealing safety data, restraining competition, and buying off influential legislators.

Not Parallel: The main character in Miller's play is conscientious, devoted, and he worked hard.

Parallel: The main character in Miller's play is conscientious, devoted, and hard-working.

CORRELATIVES

Be sure that correlatives (comparisons and contrasts like *either . . . or, neither . . . nor, not only . . . but also, both . . . and*) are followed by parallel forms.

Not Parallel: I quickly saw that my only alternatives were to run or staying and facing the consequences.

Parallel: I quickly saw that my only alternatives were to run or to stay and face the consequences.

Not Parallel: Sam was not so pleased by the huge, roaring red buses, nor even when he heard Big Ben chime the hour, as he was by one absurd little milk cart.

Parallel: Sam was not so pleased by the huge, roaring red buses, nor by Big Ben chiming the hour, as he was by one absurd little milk cart.

                         —Adapted from *Dodsworth* by Sinclair Lewis

(NOTE: To make clear a parallel construction, it may be necessary to repeat an introductory word such as a preposition, an article, or the *to* of an infinitive.)

Awkward: At the used-book sale, I bought a physics text and literature handbook.

Better: At the used-book sale, I bought a physics text and a literature handbook.

Awkward: Joan is going to the bank, and the sandal shop, but not the university.

Better: Joan is going to the bank and the sandal shop, but not to the university.

Plurals

To form the plural add *s* to the singular (*books, chairs, lights*); if the plural makes an extra syllable, add *es* (*churches, boxes, presses, flashes*). These basic rules have a number of common exceptions, which are listed below.

1. When a noun ends in *y* preceded by a *vowel,* form the plural by adding *s.*

boy	boys
toy	toys
tray	trays

When a noun ends in *y* preceded by a *consonant,* change the *y* to *i* and add *es.*

filly	fillies
travesty	travesties
army	armies

2. If a noun ends in *o* preceded by a *vowel,* form the plural by adding *s.*

studio	studios
patio	patios

If a noun ends in *o* preceded by a *consonant,* add *es.* (A few such nouns take *s* only, and a few others can take either *s* or *es.* Consult a dictionary if you are unsure.)

Negro	Negroes
echo	echoes
potato	potatoes
tomato	tomatoes

soprano	sopranos
piano	pianos
zero	zeros *or* zeroes
cargo	cargos *or* cargoes

3. When a noun ends in *f,* change the *f* to *ve* and add *s.* (*fe* becomes *ves*)

knife	knives
leaf	leaves
half	halves
thief	thieves

Some nouns that end in *f* form the regular plural.

chief	chiefs
belief	beliefs
roof	roofs

4. Some nouns, usually names of animals, have the same form for singular and plural.

fish
sheep

    trout
    deer
    salmon

5. Some nouns are used in the singular but take only plural forms.

    rabies
    physics
    economics
    measles
    mathematics

6. Most compound words are made plural by adding *s* to the last word.

    all-Americans
    rear admirals
    ex-convicts
    judge advocates

When the first word is clearly the more crucial to the meaning, however, it usually takes the *s*.

    sisters-in-law
    fathers-in-law
    governors-elect
    attorneys-at-law

Nouns ending in *ful* normally take the standard plural form.

    cupfuls
    teaspoonfuls

7. Some words have a foreign plural as well as an anglicized plural ending in *s* or *es.* The foreign plural is commonly used in technical or scientific writing. A few examples:

	Foreign Plural	Anglicized Plural
cactus	cacti	cactuses
formula	formulae	formulas

	Foreign Plural	Anglicized Plural
index	indices	indexes
radius	radii	radiuses
vertebra	vertebrae	vertebras

Certain nouns of Greek and Latin origin ending in *is* are made plural by changing *is* to *es.*

analysis	analyses
basis	bases
crisis	crises
diagnosis	diagnoses
neurosis	neuroses
parenthesis	parentheses
psychosis	psychoses
thesis	theses

Possessives

The possessive can be expressed either with an apostrophe (*Bill's, dog's, Superman's*) or with an *of* phrase (*of the book, of the building*).

POSITION OF THE APOSTROPHE

1. If the word does not end in *s,* add *'s.*

   Jim's book
   week's wages
   friend's mother
   men's hats

2. If the word ends in *s,* add an apostrophe alone. However *'s* is often added to singular nouns ending in *s,* and almost always to those ending in *ss.*

   The actress's gown
   Mr. Jones' car, or Mr. Jones's car
   The cats' (plural) food

WHICH FORM OF THE POSSESSIVE TO USE

1. Traditionally, the *'s* construction is used with living things and the *of* phrase with inanimate things (*John's home, the dog's bark, the end of the story, the top floor of the building*). This rule is by no means inflexible. In many cases, either construction could be used (*at the end of the day, at day's end*). Some idiomatic expressions take only one form (*a day's pay*, and the like).

2. If a sentence is awkward or ambiguous because of an *'s* construction, use the *of* phrase instead:

Very Awkward:	The boy down the street's house burned down yesterday.
Better:	The house of the boy down the street burned down yesterday.
Somewhat Awkward:	He could not explain the faculty and staff's motives.
Better:	He could not explain the motives of the faculty and staff.

IT'S *AND* ITS

It's is a contraction for *it is* or *it has.*
Its is the possessive form of *it.*

It's [It is] unusual for historians to confess their personal biases in their published works.

It's [It has] broken down three times already.

Its power [the power of it] is frightening.

Punctuation

APOSTROPHES

IN CONTRACTIONS. An apostrophe takes the place of one or more missing letters.

I'm (I am)	hasn't (has not)	we're (we are)
can't (cannot)	haven't (have not)	isn't (is not)
won't (will not)	it's (it is; it has)	

Contractions were once thought to be inappropriate in college papers. However, there has been a recent, though certainly not universal, movement toward the acceptance of contractions. They are acceptable in all but the most formal of college papers.

IN POSSESSIVES. See *Possessives,* p. 195.

THE COLON

Do not confuse the purpose of the colon with the purpose of the semicolon. The semicolon, like the period, *separates* elements, whereas the colon is used to *introduce.*

1. Use the colon after a statement which indicates something is to follow.

   Toad had stocked his vehicle with everything he might need: sardines, playing cards, writing paper, bacon, dominoes, and canned lobster.

2. Use the colon to introduce a long quotation.

   The letter of Charles D. Cooper was published in the newspapers: "General Hamilton has come out decidedly against Burr; indeed when he was here he spoke of him as a dangerous man and ought not to be trusted. . . . I could detail to you a still more despicable opinion which General Hamilton has expressed of Burr."

3. Use the colon in the following special situations: after the salutation in a business letter; between title and subtitle of a book; between chapter and verse in a Biblical reference; between hour and minute.

   Dear Sir:
   The Driver Ant: Unrestrained Killer
   Psalms 1:11–14
   12:01 A.M.

COMMAS

(See also *Run-On Sentences* for run-ons or comma splices.)

1. Use commas between main clauses in a compound sentence.

> The collection contains a varied set of adolescent autobiographies, but it provides too little supplementary information about the children who wrote them.

> The use of amphetamines by professional football players is increasing, and it is feared that this practice is spreading to other sports.

Commas may be omitted if the clauses are short.

> The rain fell and the wind blew.

2. Use commas after long introductory clauses or phrases, or after short ones if necessary.

> Although the moon also raises tides in the atmosphere, their effect is so slight that they will not be discussed here.

> When Shakespeare found a ready-made plot, he often built a drama around it.

> To construct a house in the expensive suburban community, you have to be prepared to spend at least $25,000 for the lot alone.

> Investigating the problem, surgeon Valdez discovered a defective plastic valve in the aorta. (Note the possible misreading if the comma is omitted.)

> To many overworked and underpaid sharecroppers, Chavez was the first to offer real hope of change.

When the modifying phrase *follows* the main clause, no commas are used if the sentence reads smoothly.

> Chavez was the first to offer real hope of change to many overworked and underpaid sharecroppers.

> Atmospheric tides will not be discussed here although they also are caused by the moon.

3. Use commas with nonrestrictive modifiers. The discussion
   below will explain the difference between restrictive and nonrestrictive clauses. These two sentences are similar but not the
   same:

   Sentence 1:   I saw the clown who was wearing red suspenders dis-
                 appear into the crowd.

   Sentence 2:   I saw the clown, who was wearing red suspenders,
                 disappear into the crowd.

The first contains a restrictive clause, or one which "restricts"
the general class "clown" to one particular clown. The second
contains the same clause, but this time it is nonrestrictive, making the meaning of the sentence slightly different. Notice that
the sentences sound different when read aloud. The two sentences can be paraphrased in this way:

   Sentence 1:   I saw a number of clowns. One of the clowns was
                 wearing red suspenders (the others were not). This
                 clown disappeared into the crowd.

   Sentence 2:   I saw one clown. He happened to be wearing red sus-
                 penders. He disappeared into the crowd.

To make the difference clearer, one might imagine a context for
each sentence:

   Sentence 1:   At the circus there were four clowns. I saw the clown
                 who was wearing red suspenders disappear into the
                 crowd.

   Sentence 2:   At the circus there was a fat lady and a clown. I saw
                 the clown, who was wearing red suspenders, disappear
                 into the crowd.

The "who" clause in the first sentence is a *restrictive clause*
(no commas). It is essential to the sentence because it distinguishes the clown who was wearing red suspenders from the
other clowns who weren't. It restricts the class of clowns to a
subject—one particular clown. In other words the clause tells

which clown. The clause in the second sentence is *nonrestric-tive* (set off by commas). The purpose of the *nonrestrictive clause* is not to differentiate one clown from another (there is only one), but to supply incidental information about that clown. Since the information is incidental, the clause is a parenthetical element, set off by commas in the way all parenthetical elements are.

a. Clauses which begin with *that* are usually *restrictive* and require no commas.

> The message that you sent was incoherent.

b. Some nouns, because they are one of a kind, cannot be restricted any further. Thus, any clause which follows such a noun would be *nonrestrictive.*

> My father, who is a religious man, never fails to attend daily mass.

> Mr. Bill Thompson, who is our Dean of Students, is away in Europe for the summer.

> Our newest boat, which is painted red and white, took its maiden voyage last weekend.

c. *Appositives,* phrases which provide incidental information, have the same function as *nonrestrictive clauses.*

> Samuel Beckett, the Irish novelist and dramatist, recently received the Nobel Prize for literature.

d. A fairly accurate way to determine whether you should use a restrictive clause or a nonrestrictive clause is to read the sentence aloud. If you read through the sentence without pause and without lowering the pitch of your voice, the clause is probably restrictive. If you pause or lower your pitch, the clause is probably nonrestrictive.

4. Use commas to set off parenthetical expressions such as

however, for example, on the other hand, and *moreover.*

> The main operation, *however,* will be performed under general anesthetic.

> *Moreover,* the Democratic Party needs to solve its financial problems.

If single word parenthetical expressions cause no hesitation when read aloud, they are best not set off by commas.

> Faulkner's finest novel is perhaps *Light in August.*

> Children certainly make better recoveries than adults with the same brain injury.

5. Use commas to separate items in a series. (If no misinterpretation is possible, the comma between the last two items is optional.)

> Baldwin wrote novels, short stories, essays, and an occasional newspaper article. (Last comma is optional.)

> Before he would make any reference to the solar explosion, he insisted on evaluating theories about the moon's origin, criticizing predictions that the moon would move closer to the earth, and presenting arguments that the sun was slowing down the earth's rotation (Last comma makes reading easier here.)

Coordinate adjectives modify the same noun. If the adjectives could be reversed, or joined by *and,* a comma should be used. If not, no comma should be used.

	He had a crafty, brilliant mind.
Also Possible:	He had a brilliant, crafty mind.
	He had a crafty and brilliant mind.
	I couldn't understand the rapid African dialect.
Impossible:	I couldn't understand the African, rapid dialect.
	I couldn't understand the African and rapid dialect.)

6. The addition of a comma is sometimes necessary to prevent a momentary misreading of a sentence. For example, try reading the following phrase without the comma:

> In the eighteenth century, institutions such as orphanages. . . .

THE DASH

The dash is used to indicate a sudden change of thought or to set off a parenthetical expression. Use the dash instead of parentheses if you want to give emphasis to the parenthetical expression. The dash can be effective, but be aware that its overuse can produce a distracting, choppy effect.

The typewritten equivalent of the dash is two hyphens with no spaces before, between, or after.

PROPER USES OF THE DASH

When I lit my candle and went up to my room that night there sat pop--his own self.--Mark Twain, The Adventures of Huckleberry Finn

It seemed to him now that they were all just shapes like chessmen--the negro, the sheriff, the money, all--unpredictable and without reason. . . .
--William Faulkner, Light in August

I know--rather I think I know--what you mean.

The persons who remember the aftermath of the first encounter can only smile sadly--it had all happened before.

THE EXCLAMATION POINT

Exclamations like ''Ouch!'' and ''My kingdom for a horse!'' rarely appear, of course, in expository prose. Avoid using the exclamation mark to add artificial emphasis. The words themselves or extra detail should carry the emphasis.

Instead of

He was stupid and vicious!

a writer can say

He was a stupid, vicious man, capable of sending his friends to the gallows and innocent children to prison.

PARENTHESES

Parentheses are used to enclose supplementary or explanatory material.

> Each essay should range between three and five typewritten pages or their handwritten equivalent (roughly 700 to 1200 words), excluding the pages needed for footnotes and bibliography.

Don't allow parentheses to become stylistic crutches. Set off material with parentheses only when absolutely necessary. Sentences will look better and read easier if the material is integrated.

Awkward: Mr. Smith (Teddy's father) seemed to delight in scolding Teddy (even though Teddy rarely did anything wrong).

Better: Mr. Smith seemed to delight in scolding his son Teddy, even though the boy rarely did anything wrong.

PARENTHESES AND BRACKETS. Do not confuse the use of parentheses with the use of brackets. Parentheses enclose explanatory remarks in your own writing. Brackets enclose explanatory remarks you wish to insert in quoted material.

> Of professional football players, Bartley Horwitz (in *Pro Football: Big Business*) says, "Many [of the Green Bay Packers] have used their professional careers as stepping-stones to lucrative business jobs."

PARENTHESES WITH FIGURES AND LETTERS. Parentheses are used to enclose figures or letters that comprise a list.

> The authors present strong evidence to support their assertions that (1) education is used to raise rather than lower barriers between people, (2) the government has resisted all attempts to reverse this policy, (3) tax money raised from those with lower incomes subsidizes education for wealthier groups, and (4) poorer people are becoming increasingly restive about the educational system.

PUNCTUATION WITH PARENTHESES

1. If the parentheses come within a sentence, punctuate as if the parentheses were not there; that is, the punctuation should go *outside* the parentheses.

> Voting against the bill was Clinton Anderson.

> Voting against the bill was Clinton Anderson (Democrat, New Mexico).

2. If the parenthetical material is a complete sentence in itself, punctuation should go *inside* the parentheses.

> (Voting against the bill was Clinton Anderson.)

THE PERIOD

1. Use a period at the end of statements, indirect questions, and mildly imperative sentences, or those which are not exclamations.

Statement:	It has been necessary to reduce the amount of the fellowships.
Indirect Question:	He asked if it had been necessary to reduce the amount of the fellowships.
Mild Imperative:	Find out if it has been necessary to reduce the amount of the fellowships.

2. Use a period after most abbreviations. See p. 171, *Abbreviations*.

3. Use three spaced periods to indicate an omission (an ellipsis) in quoted material. See p. 205, under *Quotation Marks*.

THE QUESTION MARK

Use a question mark at the end of every direct (not indirect) question.

Direct:	What is the purpose of your visit?
Indirect:	He asked what the purpose of your visit was.

(NOTE: It is generally a poor practice to make statements by asking questions of your reader. He may be irritated by such rhetorical questions because they seem unnecessary, contrived, even condescending.)

Unnecessary Question:	What is the theme of Frost's poem, ''The Pasture''? The theme of the poem is the simple expression that the beauty of nature is better enjoyed by two people than by one person alone.
Concise Statement:	''The Pasture'' by Robert Frost makes the simple proposition that the beauty of nature is better enjoyed by two people than by one person alone.

QUOTATION MARKS

WHEN TO USE QUOTATION MARKS

1. Use quotation marks only to enclose the *exact* words spoken or written by someone. You should not use quotation marks for an *indirect* quotation since the exact words are not reproduced.

   Direct: She said, ''It's cold today.''

   Indirect: She said that it's cold today.

2. Quotation marks are also used to enclose the titles of magazines and newspaper articles, songs, poems, and short stories.

   ''White Rabbit,'' by the Jefferson Airplane.

   ''Aspirin: Is It Addictive?'' reprinted in *Today's Medicine.*

3. Sometimes you may use quotation marks to exhibit a mocking tone.

   This ''man of honor'' became rich by peddling worthless stocks to small investors.

   or to show that you are using an informal word in a formal context:

   In the room were found large quantities of barbiturates or ''reds.''

Notice that the quotation marks in the above sentence mean, in effect, ''I am quoting the language of another group or another context. These are not, at this time, really my own words.''

4. Fight the tendency to put quotation marks around words of your own. In a few years, sentences like the one below have a dated sound, making the writer appear somewhat foolish:

> Billy was really ''cute.'' All the ''chicks'' wanted to date him.

If you are tempted to use quotation marks in this way, ask yourself why you need them. If you are apologizing for slang or a cliché, rewrite the sentence so that the need for quotation marks is eliminated.

5. If, on the other hand, you still want to use the expression in question, then use it but don't use the quotation marks. Don't apologize with quotation marks if it's your own word, your language, and it's what you want to say.

HOW TO USE QUOTATION MARKS

1. When quotation marks are required *within* a quotation, use single quotation marks.

> Joan said, ''Yes, I heard 'Light My Fire,' but I can't seem to remember the words.''

> Mr. Jones said, ''I remember Roosevelt's words, 'The only thing to fear is fear itself.' ''

2. If a quotation continues for more than one paragraph, that is, if the same speaker speaks for two or three paragraphs, use quotation marks at the beginning of every paragraph but at the end of only the last.

3. To quote dialogue, use a separate paragraph for every change of speaker.

> ''Another brandy,'' he said, pointing to the glass. The waiter who was in a hurry came over.
>
> ''Finished,'' he said, speaking with that omission of syntax stupid

people employ when talking to drunken people or foreigners. "No more tonight. Close now."

"Another," said the old man.

"No. Finished."—Ernest Hemingway, *A Clean Well Lighted Place*

PUNCTUATION BEFORE A QUOTATION

1. If the quotation is very short and emphatic, no punctuation is needed.

    The coach yelled "Shoot!" when the clock had run down to only three seconds.

2. A comma should precede a short quotation.

    Bill replied, "This omission stands out as the main deficiency in his theory."

3. A colon should precede a long quotation.

    One critic compares the two novels: "Just as *The Red Badge of Courage* is not a religious novel, neither is *Sister Carrie* concerned with the morality of man's actions. Like Crane, Dreiser interjects no heavy-handed preaching, either in direct commentary or through his characters. Both novels are decidedly amoral."

    (Also see *Footnotes,* p. 97.)

PUNCTUATION AFTER A QUOTATION

1. Periods and commas are always placed inside the quotation marks.

    "I know," he said, "but I still can't wait."

    After the lecture he had but one comment: "Useless."

    The following words are mispelled in your paper: "tediously," "experiment," and "usury."

2. Colons and semicolons always go outside the quotation marks.

    All he says is, "Please pass the sugar"; perhaps those are the only words he knows.

There are two points worth remembering in the article "Skin Diving at Hanauma Bay": you should never attempt to cross the reef at low tide and you should avoid the rip tide just outside the cove.

3. Question marks, exclamation marks, and dashes are placed inside the quotation marks if they apply to the quotation only—that is, if they are a part of the quotation itself.

Ed threw down the book and yelled, "Don't bother me!" (Only the quotation is an exclamation.)

I picked up the book and asked him, "When may I talk with you without bothering you?" (Only the quotation is a question.)

They are placed outside the quotation marks if they apply to the sentence as a whole; that is, if they are *not* a part of the quotation itself.

Was it Mr. Pickwick who said, "If the law says that, sir, then the law's an ass"? (The entire statement is a question.)

When will you get it through your head that I don't want anyone ever to say "Please"! (The entire statement is an exclamation.)

LONG QUOTATIONS. If a quotation is less than four or five lines you may quote it without modification within the body of the paragraph. If it is longer than four or five lines, however, you should separate the quotation from the paragraph, indent five spaces for each line, and use single spacing. When a quotation is in this "block form," quotation marks should be omitted.

Both as a critic and as a writer, Virginia Woolf shared in the artistic concern for realizing the best artistic form into which a writer translates the matter of reality. She realized that art implies order, selection, and arrangement; her novels were cohesive and tightly controlled, and in statements of criticism she argued for adherence to literary standards.

If fiction is, as we suggest, in difficulties, it may be because nobody grasps her firmly and defines her severely. She has had no rules drawn up for her, very little thinking done on her behalf. And though rules may be wrong and must be broken, they have this advantage—they

confer dignity and order upon their subject; they admit her to a place
in civilized society; they prove that she is worthy of distinction.

—''The Art of Fiction''

VERSE

Verse may be quoted within the body of the paragraph if it is
no more than two lines. A line break is indicated by a diagonal
line (/).

''This above all: to thine own self be true,'' Polonius advised his
son Laertes. ''And it must follow, as the night the day/ Thou
canst not then be false to any man.''

If the verse is more than two lines, you should quote it exactly as it appears in the original, indented and single spaced.

The chorus contrasts Dionysus, born of Zeus, to the ''rabid beast''
Pentheus:

With fury, with fury he rages,
Pentheus, son of Echion,
born of the breed of Earth,
spawned by the dragon, whelped by earth!
Inhuman, a rabid beast.

—Euripides, *The Bacchae* (tr. William Arrowsmith)

INSERTIONS AND OMISSIONS IN QUOTATIONS

BRACKETS. If you want to clarify or explain a part of a quotation,
your insertions should be enclosed with brackets. For example, in
the following quotation it might be unclear to your reader who
''He'' refers to:

''He was one of the first defenders of the theory of natural
selection.''

Clarified: ''[Huxley] was one of the first defenders of the theory of natural selection.''

ELLIPSES. An ellipsis is a punctuation mark of three spaced periods which indicates that a part of the quotation has been omitted.

If an ellipsis comes at the end of the sentence, you should use four spaced periods (the period at the end of the sentence in addition to the ellipsis).

> "It is important to analyse the methods by which Virginia Woolf worked out her critical theories. . . . *To the Lighthouse* . . . is an excellent model from which to work. . . ."

Many student writers needlessly preface quotations. For example,

> Sartre acknowledges the perpetual conflict which is the only possible outcome of human relations. He does so in the following quotation: "Everything which may be said of me in my relations with the Other applies to him as well. While I attempt to free myself from the hold of the Other, the Other is trying to free himself from mine; while I seek to enslave the Other, the Other seeks to enslave me."

The sentence, "He does so in the following quotation," is unnecessary and should be omitted. The reader knows that the quotation relates directly to the sentence preceding it. There is no need to point out the connection.

(NOTE: Do not use "quote" as a noun, as in "He used too many quotes in his paper." Use "quotation" instead.)

THE SEMICOLON

In most cases you should use a semicolon only where you could have used a period, or a conjunction like *and, but, or, nor, however,* or *therefore.* Ordinarily the semicolon, like the period, is used to separate main clauses. Because the semicolon is not as strong a break as the period, however, you can use the semicolon between main clauses that are closely related.

> Measham's book provides a thoughtful analysis of the problem of pain; the importance of his research can hardly be overstated.

1. A semicolon may separate any two main clauses, provided that they are not already separated by a coordinate conjunction (*and, or, but, nor*).

Incorrect: Jensen's work was welcomed by opponents of bussing; and they made no attempt to check the reliability of the evidence.

Correct: Jensen's work was welcomed by opponents of bussing; they made no attempt to check the reliability of the evidence.

Correct: It has been alleged that the Puritans felt a monstrous guilt for separating from their mother country; this guilt was probably little in comparison to the awesome responsibility they must have borne as they, the last best hope for mankind, sailed for an unknown wilderness to reconcile humanity with God.

Correct: Hawthorne is often criticized for his use of allegory; many of his literary devices take on no meaning other than a singular representation of one idea or thing.

2. The semicolon is placed before a coordinate conjunction if the first main clause already contains commas or is unusually long.

   Jensen's work, based on dubious statistical evidence, was welcomed by opponents of bussing; and they made no attempt to check the reliability of the evidence.

3. The semicolon is sometimes needed to prevent confusion in a sentence that contains many commas.

   Confusing: The following persons perished in the shipwreck: Black Bart, a conniving pirate, Ensign Jones, Billy McTeague, the cabin boy and Commodore Faddle.
   [How many died? Six? Five? Four?]

   Clear: The following persons perished in the shipwreck: Black Bart, a conniving pirate; Ensign Jones; Billy McTeague, the cabin boy; and Commodore Faddle.

4. Note that semicolons should separate only elements that are of equal rank: two main clauses, two subordinate clauses, or two phrases.

Run-on Sentences

A run-on sentence consists of two sentences improperly joined. For example, the following are joined with only a comma,

> The boy became ill, he went home.

an error sometimes labeled ''comma splice.''
These are joined with no punctuation at all:

> The boy became ill he went home.

The run-on is a liability to good writing because it may be confusing and difficult to read. These are a number of simple ways to correct the run-on.

1. Place a period at the end of the first sentence and capitalize the first word of the second.

    > The boy became ill. He went home.

2. Place a semicolon between the two parts (if they are closely related in content).

    > The boy became ill; he went home.

3. Place the proper conjunction between the two sentences, making one compound sentence.

    > The boy became ill and (he) went home.

4. Subordinate one of the sentences, making one complex sentence.

    > Because the boy became ill, he went home.

Admittedly, many run-on sentences are usually not as easy to diagnose as our simple illustration. Nevertheless, no matter how long or involved two consecutive sentences may be, they must be joined, or separated, correctly. Of the four possible ways to correct a run-on, one is usually preferable to the other three. Take the following run-on sentence as an example:

> Many women are more vehement than men in opposing the extension of legal rights to their own sex, they have the same cultural biases as the male chauvinists.

Possible corrections:

1. Place a conjunction between the two sentences. This remedy, to make a compound sentence out of the run-on, would be grammatically correct but illogical.

   > Many women are more vehement than men in opposing the extension of legal rights to their own sex, *and* they have the same cultural biases as the male chauvinists.

2. Place a period at the end of the first sentence and capitalize the first word of the second. This correction is both grammatical and logical. The connection between ideas in the two sentences is implied not stated.

   > Many women are more vehement than men in opposing the extension of legal rights to their own sex. They have the same cultural biases as the male chauvinists.

3. Place a semicolon between the two sentences. This correction has virtually the same advantages as the one immediately above. Moreover the use of the semicolon rather than a period suggests a close logical linking. This correction is probably the best here.

4. Subordinate one of the sentences. This remedy is grammatical, logical, and states clearly the connection between the related ideas in the two sentences.

   > Many women are more vehement than men in opposing the extension of legal rights to their own sex *because* they have the same cultural biases as the male chauvinists.

Sentence Fragments

A fragment is an incomplete sentence. It may be incomplete because it lacks either a subject or a predicate.

But to combat this feeling of hysteria.

In the clutches of the sea monster.

Hoping to change my major.

If a string of words has a subject and a predicate, but is introduced by a relative pronoun (*who, which, that*) or a subordinating conjunction (such as *although, when, if, because*), it still is a fragment:

Even though I marked all the boxes with an X.

Which sounds more interesting every time I hear it.

HOW TO CORRECT FRAGMENTS

If the fragment belongs with either the sentence before it or the one after it, make the appropriate connection.

Fragment: *Being afraid of the dark.* I frequently was unable to sleep.

Sentence: Being afraid of the dark, I frequently was unable to sleep.

Fragment: He respected DuBois. *Because he used language as if it were the last desperate weapon of the Black mind.*

Sentence: He respected DuBois because he used language as if it were the last desperate weapon of the Black mind.

You may choose to rewrite the fragment, inserting the necessary subject and predicate.

Fragment: *Hoping to attend the W. C. Fields festival.*

Sentence: I hoped to attend the W. C. Fields festival.

PASSAGES CONTAINING FRAGMENTS

Our arrival caused quite a stir in the sleepy Mexican fishing town. *The small children shouting in their foreign tongue while their bigger brothers and sisters silently stood by watching.*

Revised: Our arrival caused quite a stir in the sleepy Mexican fishing town. The small children shout*ed* in their foreign tongue while their bigger brothers and sisters silently stood by watching.

During the next two centuries conditions changed sufficiently to lead the Spanish monarchs to petition the Pope for a tribunal to aid in the investigation and punishment of heresy. *In hope of solidifying their control and guaranteeing the orthodoxy of the Spanish Church.*

During the next two centuries conditions changed sufficiently to lead the Spanish monarchs to petition the Pope for a tribunal to aid in the investigation and punishment of heresy. *They hoped to solidify* their control and *guarantee* the orthodoxy of the Spanish Church.

Spelling

Consult the dictionary for words you are in doubt about. Also learn, if you don't already know them, these general patterns of English words.

PREFIXES

Prefixes like *dis-, pre-,* and *re-* are simply attached.

dis . . . position	in . . . consistent
dis . . . appoint	in . . . coherent
pre . . . cede	in . . . numerable
pre . . . view	in . . . audible
re . . . instate	in . . . discriminate

The prefix *in-* changes before the sounds, *m, r* and *l.*

ir . . . reverent	im . . . measurable
ir . . . responsible	il . . . legal

SUFFIXES

Suffixes like *-able* and *-ment* and verb endings *-ed* and *-ing* are usually just added on:

bark . . . ing	walk . . . ed

```
base . . . ment          rent . . . able
cautious . . . ness      sure . . . ly
```

But a final *e* on a root word drops off if the suffix begins with a vowel:

```
crave        crav . . . ing
dive         div . . . ing
retrieve     retriev . . . ing
```

The final *e* serves to show the length of the vowel—the long *a* in *tape* rather than the short *a* in *tap*. If another vowel can take the place of the *e*, like the *i* in *-ing*, then the *e* is dropped, and you have *taping*. With words like *tap*, where the vowel is short, an extra consonant has to be inserted to keep it short, hence *tap-p-ing*.

EXCEPTION. The sound of soft *c* and soft *g*, however, require an *e* or an *i* after them to keep them soft; *ci* and *ce* are soft *c* sounds, but *co, ca,* and *cu* are hard sounds. Thus:

Keep the *e* in *noticeable* to keep the *c* soft.

Keep the *e* in *courageous* to keep the *g* soft.

THE y *AND THE* i

Words ending in *y* often change the *y* to *i*.

1. Change *y* to *i* and add *es:*

```
candy . . . . . . candies
lady . . . . . . . ladies
```

2. Change *y* to *i* and add *-al* or *-ness:*

```
deny . . . . . . denial
lovely . . . . . loveliness
```

3. Don't change *y* to *i* if, by doing so, you would produce a double *i* or a strange-looking string of three vowels:

valleys	(not vall*ei*es)
toys	(not to*i*es)
rays	(not ra*i*es)
staying	(not sta*i*ing)
relying	(not reli*i*ng)
dying	(not d*i*ing)

(NOTE: *Skiing* is the only exception.)

THE i *AND THE* e

The old rule is still the best:

i before *e*:	*field, friend, grief*
except after *c*:	*receipt, perceive, deceive*

and when sounded like *ay* as in "neighbor" and "weigh":

freight, deign, heir, feign

(Also *height,* which doesn't sound like *ay*).
EXCEPTIONS: *leisure, weird, seize*

Split Infinitives

It is usually awkward to split an infinitive—*to walk,* or *to communicate*—by slipping an adverb between the *to* and the verb:

to *effectively* communicate
to *gracefully* walk

Better to say:

to communicate effectively
to walk gracefully

Occasionally a writer's language sense, however, tells him that it is better to split an infinitive than not to split it. Earlier in this book we wrote about a writer's lack of control over his prose. We said that such a lack of control

results from the author's apparent unwillingness to think,
to really think, about McLuhan's ideas.

To decide whether it would have been better to write:

really to think

we read it aloud both ways and decided to split the infinitive.

Word Division

You should only need to break a word if the lines at the right-hand
margin of your paper would otherwise be unusually ragged. A
wide right-hand margin can accommodate all but the most lengthy
words. In the event that a word must be broken, follow these
rules.

1. The hyphen should be placed at the end of a line, not the beginning of the following line.

2. Break words only in between syllables.

butter-cup	*not*	butte-rcup
im-plicate	*not*	impl-icate

   Obviously, one-syllable words cannot be broken

through	*not*	thr-ough
flipped	*not*	flip-ped

   nor can short words like *cheery* and *ferry.* You cannot break between every syllable in a longer word.

3. There should be at least two letters in a syllable to set it off
   from the rest of the word.

ador-able	*not*	a-dorable
elusive-ness	*not*	e-lusiveness

4. Words already hyphenated should be broken only at the hyphen.

self-assurance	*not*	self-assur-ance
ex-convict	*not*	ex-con-vict

5. In words containing double consonants, break in between the double consonants rather than just before or after them.

stop-ping	*not*	stopp-ing

6. When two different consonants occur together in a long word, they may be separated but only if the breaking does not interfere with natural pronunciation.

in-spire	*not*	ins-pire
de-flect	*not*	def-lect

7. You can usually place a hyphen before *-ing.* But you should not separate *-ble* from its root word:

drink-able	*not*	drinka-ble

Index

Margin Symbols

ab	Unnecessary abbreviation	Abbreviation, p. 171
agr	Agreement	Agreement: Subject and Verb, p. 174; Agreement: Pronoun and Antecedent, p. 178
awk, k	Awkward sentence	Monster Sentences, p. 136; Overnominalization in Sentences, p. 120; Parallelism, p. 190
cap	Capital	Capitals, p. 180
cliché	Overused, empty expression	Clichés, p. 164
coh	Not coherent: sentences do not lead easily from one to the next; reader loses sense of focus or direction	Incoherence, p. 14
colloq	Colloquial language where the content demands more formal language	Colloquial English, p. 166
def	Undefined terms	Undefined Terms, p. 22
dev	Idea should be further developed	Paragraph Development, p. 30
focus	Lack of focus, or sense of direction; reader feels lost, and does not know what you are aiming at	Unifying Idea, p. 30; Sample Approaches and Papers, p. 66
frag	Sentence fragment	Sentence Fragments, p. 213
ftnt	Footnote needed	Footnotes, p. 97
inf	Split infinitive	Split Infinitive, p. 217
intro, con	Introduction, conclusion	Beginning and Ending Paragraphs, p. 32
jarg	Inflated, excessively complex language	Jargon, p. 148
lc	Lower case	Capitals, p. 180
mm	Mixed metaphor	Mistakes with Metaphor, p. 163
overgen	Overgeneralizing; broad claims not justified	Overgeneralization, p. 16
oversimp	Oversimplification of a complex idea or problem	Oversimplification, p. 20
p	Punctuation	Punctuation, p. 197
¶ (no ¶)	Should (should not) be a new paragraph.	
para (⫽)	Parallel structure	Parallelism, p. 190
plot sum	Tendency to do no more than summarize the plot when writing about a novel or a play	Relevance, p. 10; Literature Sample Paper, p. 71
poss	Possessive form; use of apostrophe	Possessives, p. 195
pro	Mistake with *I, me, who, whom*	Pronoun Forms, p. 130